Fighting
For Freedom
And Fun

Fighting For Freedom And Fun

by

Major Michael Pope, M.C.

with a Foreword by
Major Dick Hern, C.V.O., C.B.E.

TIGER & TYGER LIMITED
7 Lower Grosvenor Place
London SW1

PUBLISHED IN THE UK BY
TIGER & TYGER LTD
7 Lower Grosvenor Place
London SW1

DISTRIBUTED BY
THOMAS LYSTER LTD
Unit 9 ~ Ormskirk Industrial Park
Old Boundary Way
Burscough Road
Ormskirk
Lancashire L39 2YW
Tel: 01695 575112
Fax: 01695 570120

First Published 1999
© Michael Pope 1999
ISBN 1 902914 01 5

BY THE SAME AUTHOR

All Such Fun
More Fun and Frolic
Barrels of Fun

Contents

Foreword by Dick Hern   i

Introduction by Michael Pope   iii

Chapter 1	A Hunting We Will Go	1
Chapter II	Hooked on Horses	10
Chapter III	Call to Arms	20
Chapter IV	Officers and Gentlemen	24
Chapter V	The Battle for Longstop Hill	34
Chapter VI	The Battle of the Hitler Line	49
Chapter VII	The War is Over	60
Chapter VIII	Entente Cordiale	77
Chapter IX	Back to Blighty	83
	Aftermath of War	89
Appendix 1	The author's MC Citation	90
Appendix 2	Kaiser Bill	91
Appendix 3	Jam Omelettes	92
Index		93

Foreword

BY DICK HERN

When Michael Pope asked me to write the foreword to his book, I was really delighted. He and I have been best friends for over fifty years and without his help and encouragement there is no doubt that I would have found it very difficult, I should say impossible, to get into the racing game, and certainly would not have become private trainer to the late Major L.B. Holliday in 1957 which gave me the opportunity and experience of training some high class horses.

This book is the story of a young man who was fascinated by horses and of his life just before the War and an account of his time in the Army in Algeria, Tunisia and Italy and, subsequently, his launch into a training career – of which I was a part from 1952 to 1957 when I was his assistant trainer.

i

I am sure that those who read it will be unable to put it down as his powers of description are always so vivid.

When I was Michael's assistant I was treated like one of the family by his parents and brothers and it was the greatest fun. Nearly all his owners were personal friends and raced entirely for sport. Many of them liked to have a punt and celebrated their victories in style, and this made my time with him all the more exciting.

It was a unique set up and how fortunate I was to be part of it, before everything in racing became so commercial.

Those were happy days!

Introduction

BY MICHAEL POPE

Forgive me if I should appear to write of war in light-hearted tones. My intention is to smoke-screen the deeper horrors of the battlefields.

For me war is the greatest curse of mankind and at the end of the day those involved must surely regret their actions.

I fought hard reluctantly, and it was a fight for survival. The deeds of daring attributed to me were none other than in defence of myself and those unfortunates under my care.

We were fighting for freedom to live the life of our choice and do not take kindly to the threats posed to liberty to this day.

All of us were desperate to stay alive but some were luckier than others. My family were fortunate in having been dealt a nap hand, with all four brothers, Peter, Patrick, Barrington and myself returning home unscathed. Maybe our lucky charm played a part (see Appendix 2, page 91).

Sadly so many of our close comrades perished and were left behind in the burial grounds of North Africa and Italy, bringing tragic grief to their families and loved ones. This book is in part a tribute to them.

Chapter One

A HUNTING WE WILL GO

Education permitting, my twin brother Patrick and I seldom missed an opportunity to go hunting with our local pack of hounds, the Puckeridge Hunt. Their kennels are at Much Hadham, home of the Barclays, a large family of sporting farmers who have provided the Hunt Master for a hundred years and more. Only recently there was a grand centennial anniversary to mark the occasion.

To say we went hunting is something of an exaggeration because, as youngsters, we never really became as fully involved in the sport or as deeply as we would have liked. Our family groom, Mr. Marshall, always escorted us, making sure we remained towards the back of the field even when a fox had been found and hounds were in full cry. Maybe he imagined he was guarding the safety of our steeds as well as his job. More likely, Marshall was windy and feared his footy old cob would bury him if he attempted to leave the ground.

The thrilling cry of those hounds speaking with such delight across open country, urged on by the Huntsman blowing his horn, gave us a frantic desire to break free and join in the chase, jumping all manner of obstacles as we kicked on fearlessly. Likewise, our ponies, with hearts thumping, ears twitching and flanks quivering, were clearly bursting to be given their heads. But Marshall restrained us to a sharp canter, reining back to a walk when passing through open gates or gaps in the hedgerows, rather than encouraging us to jump even the most feeble obstacles.

Just before Christmas 1930 our old man, Alec, an extremely generous person at any time but even more so having landed a nice touch on the horses at Sandown with The Masher and The Bastard announced out of the blue: "Now then young lads, what would you like most for Christmas?" Nudging Pat, confident he would agree with the request I was about to make on our behalf, I ventured: "A day's hunting on Boxing Day without Marshall in attendance."

No doubt surprised we had not asked for something like a Whippy saddle or new pony apiece, he replied: "A very reasonable request. You're both rising fourteen, the age of puberty, and are old enough and ugly enough to hunt your own prey without restraint, whether it be females or foxes."

Although it was more than sixty-five years ago, I remember that Boxing Day as if it were yesterday. The bitch pack were to meet at Little Hallingbury Hall, only a short hack through Hatfield Forest, close by our parents' home at Thremhall Priory, a charming old Georgian house with a grand little stable yard. It was a bright, crisp, frosty morning with a smattering of snow on the ground, but hopefully not enough to deprive us of the hunting we had longed for.

Pat and I were out of bed at sparrow fart and in the stables wisping over our two freshly clipped ponies, Ginger and Mollie, both chestnuts just under fifteen hands and therefore referred to rather insultingly as 'ponies'. We plaited their manes without a hair awry and greased their feet with neatsfoot oil. Pat put a tail bandage on his mare, while I adorned my gelding's tail with a red ribbon, as he was prone to kick hounds. Besides, I reckoned it lent a more professional touch to the turn-out.

Leaving them tacked up we returned to the house for a hearty breakfast. Our mother Tim, whom we all loved dearly and addressed by her nickname, was as excited as we when she tied our stocks and checked that we were presentably attired. Her Christmas present to

2

us had been dark blue hunting caps from Harry Hall and a 'long tom' apiece with our initials inscribed on a silver band around the handle. Believe it or not mine still hangs in the front hall for use when I go hunting stray cats with my pack of Jack Russells!

The author on Dormitory at the gates of Thremhall Priory, his parents' home.

Returning to the yard we straightened our horses' tack and climbed aboard. When leaving the stables we lied through our teeth to Marshall, saying how sorry we were he was not coming with us. Allowing plenty of time we hacked on quietly through the forest, picking the best of the going to avoid spoiling our turn-outs. Of course, we knew the forest like the back of our hands, having exercised there practically every day. It was ideal hacking country with wide rides through the wooded areas where we had erected various obstacles for schooling and pretend racing with our chums.

One such ride ended at Fanny Carter's cottage door. She was a wonderful old Irish character who sold home-made sweets through her kitchen window: delicious toffee, chocolate fudge, humbugs and

3

gobstoppers. Her speciality was coconut ice – white, pink, brown and green, all creamy and gooey. In fact, irresistible. Fanny had only one tooth in her head, loose and as black as night. When we enquired how it was she made such delectable sweets the answer, in all seriousness, would be: "Well it's like this luv, I do 'ave a sweet toot."

When she was asked how old she was, a wry grin would come over her wrinkled face: "I do lose count after my ninety-fifth birthday." The old character had a stinking nanny-goat called Gertie, also a ripe old age, but still producing the creamy milk used in the sweet making and possibly the secret ingredient that made the coconut ice so very special. Gertie was also a strong deterrent to intruders entering the cottage garden. Pat and I never attempted to venture beyond the gate. Rumour had it that interlopers had been seen leaving with tears in their eyes, and clutching their private parts, having suffered a painful butting by Gertie.

Apologies for digressing from the hunting scene, but sadly one meets very few Fanny Carters in one's lifetime, and even fewer able to make such delicious coconut ice!

We cast up at the park gates as the church bells struck eleven o'clock. There, sitting astride a powerful dapple grey hunter, with hounds gathered around him, was the Master himself, Major Maurice Barclay, known as Mo and regarded with reverential awe by all. To our amazement, as we were passing by, he raised his silver goblet filled either with sloe gin or cherry brandy, to say, "Morning young fellas, welcome to your first real hunt and congratulations to mounts and riders on their turn-out." Spotting the sartorial red ribbon on Ginger's tail he added, "But heaven help you if that chestnut nag kicks my hounds!"

Clearly, he must have been primed by the Hunt Secretary of the fact that we had been given our

4

freedom from Marshall via Tim when she paid the 'caps' on our behalf. Any further conversation with Major Barclay was quashed when Nellie, the Duchess of Hitchcock, came thundering along on an elephant of a cob, resplendent with hogged mane, docked tail and the quarters of a Suffolk Punch, not dissimilar to those of the Duchess! Nellie was a vast lady with powerful bosoms, a moustache and voice like a foghorn. A chain smoker, she was seldom seen without a Balkan Sobranie hanging from the corner of her mouth. Hence the nickname Nicotine Nelly, by which she was affectionately known to her staff. With a graveyard cough she roared in dark brown tones, "Mornin' Master Mo. I'd prefer if you didn't draw Home Covert in the park this morning, 'cause the Duke gave me a champion Burmese moggy for Christmas and when the footman put him out for a stale before we hit the sack the handsome beast pushed off and keeper Harris reported he saw him crossing the ride when he was feeding pheasants this morning. I don't doubt your half-starved bitches would soon have him for breakfast."

Although a demanding lady, both the Duchess and her old man were seriously generous subscribers to the hunt. Furthermore, they owned a large slice of very sporting country and to have ignored their wishes would be foolhardy. The Master turned to his huntsman and said, "Did you hear that Jock, Her Grace's cat is loose?"

Jock replied, "Aye, aye Master, but I thought all cats were loose." Thinking it wise to ignore such an indelicate quip, the Master gestured his Huntsman to blow hounds for move off.

Pat and I pulled over on the grass verge bordering the wide drive to allow hounds to pass by. I aimed Ginger's quarters at a thick rhododendron bush for fear he might be in a kicking mood. Following on after the

5

hounds and Master came three or four snooty-looking gentlemen, who clearly considered themselves socially superior. In pink coats and polished top hats, they chatted up equally precious-looking ladies, riding side saddle and dressed to kill. Their facial appearances were camouflaged and in most cases enhanced by eye-veils masking their faces. Large bunches of sweet-smelling parma violets pinned to their lapels added further grandeur.

Immediately behind the so-called elite came a horde of assorted followers, whose only intention was to enjoy the sport of foxhunting. Among those mounted were a healthy number of sporting farmers over whose land we hunted, and without whose co-operation the hunt would not exist.

Just such a farmer was Monty Rose, a jolly old character with ruddy complexion and expensive nose to match. A very valuable member of the hunt, he knew the country well and had a canny knack of sensing where a fox would break covert. Such knowledge was invaluable. He always had a couple of blood horses to qualify with the Puckeridge and frequently won the members race at the point-to-point.

His daughter Marigold, a skilful and gutsy rider, was rather plump and certainly no oil painting. However, there was something about her that caught the eye. Possibly her tantalising bottom, moulded into a pair of skin-tight breeches and only partially covered by her bum-freezer jacket. A rare treat which Pat and I surreptitiously admired from the rear where we always attempted to position ourselves.

The Master made sure Home Covert was duly given a wide berth, and the Huntsman took hounds to a likely-looking plantation on the other side of the park, adjacent to the boundary wall. We spotted Monty and daughter cantering off on their own along to the far end of the wood to take up point duty to spot the fox as he left the wood. Pat and I decided to follow on to watch hounds working from afar. It wasn't long before a couple started to give tongue. The scent was obviously good and quite quickly the entire pack joined the cry.

Suddenly, we spotted a big red dog fox with a handsome brush sneak out of the undergrowth where Monty and Marigold stood on the bank. He made his way nonchalantly through a gap in the wall and on into a narrow strip of sunflowers, planted solely as feed for the pheasants. Monty, standing erect in his irons with bowler hat held aloft, let out an ear-piercing view halloa. Purple in the face he continued to roar like a man possessed. The leading hound soon broke covert, closely followed by three or four more until the entire pack had checked in the lane to pick up the scent and, with muzzles to the ground, streamed on into the game crop.

The Huntsman soon appeared, galloping furiously along the lane, blowing away on his horn like blazes with his whipper-in calling hounds onto the line. "Hi on there Bitchy, hi in there Harmony, get on there Melody." The uproar reached a crescendo as pheasants flushed in every direction. What luck we decided to tail Monty and Marigold and so witness such an exhilarating scene!

Once out of the sunflowers the fox could be seen streaking away over the hill across open country with hounds in close pursuit. The sound of the horn blowing, hounds screaming and halloas in the distance sent shivers down our spines. Urging the ponies on, we could see the lead riders kicking on into an inviting-looking obstacle. As we got closer we saw it was a neatly slashed hawthorn hedge, not too high but plenty wide and thick. Some horses were standing off and leaping like stags, others propped and scotched before scrambling over, while a few stuck their toes in and decanted their pilots. Just then Marigold steamed

7

upsides and shouted, "Kick on lads, follow me, I'll give you a lead."

Unaware of the big drop on the landing side of the fence, we were both left behind. But with feet stuck well forward and reins slipped to the buckle, we touched down in one piece and kicked on to catch up Marigold and get a good view from behind. The hunt continued fast and furious for an hour or more. We jumped or scrambled over every sort of fence from post and rails, cut and laid hedges to ditches and gates.

Pat and I had both suffered a couple of falls, with no real harm to man or beast, but our ponies were very tired and as other horsemen changed to their second horses we decided to call it a day. Just then, away in the distance, we could hear a horn blowing 'Gone to ground'. Over the brow of the hill we could see a small bunch of riders down in the valley, mostly in pink and dismounted amidst clouds of steam from their sweating horses. On getting closer, the note of the horn, the sound of yapping, hunt terriers and baying hounds, told us there had been a kill.

As we rode up and dismounted, the huntsman was removing the mask and brush before tossing the remainder of the carcass to the hounds. The Master then called across towards us, "Come on forrad lads, what better day to take home a trophy of your first real hunt," and with that handed me the brush and Patrick the mask. With this honour bestowed we decided to head for home. Having loosened girths we dismounted and led Ginger and Mollie back down the lane, which we were assured would eventually bring us to the forest and home. It was a fair old trek and nearly dark when we spotted the welcoming lights of our stable yard. Marshall was there to greet us and sportingly said: "I'll see to the ponies, you get on indoors for a warm up. The thrills and spills of today can wait till mornin'."

Tim had helped Ada, our large and jolly family cook, to prepare our favourite high tea: handfuls of lightly boiled eggs with oodles of freshly baked bread and home made butter.

For afters there was Tim's famous cake, laden with fruit, dipped in the middle, all soggy, gooey and still hot from the oven. Ada used to say, "That indigestible tackle will be the death of you lads." I'm now four-score years and still there is none to make a cake quite like old Tim. God bless her. Without doubt that was one of the best days of our lives and after a soak in the bath we went to kip early, tired, sore and bruised. But very, very happy.

Chapter Two

HOOKED ON HORSES

We were now addicted to the sport of foxhunting, although since we were at college our sport was restricted to a couple of half days per week during the season. However, to become serious followers we needed to replace our faithful and brave ponies with a couple of nags with more scope, size and speed. Sadly, but fortuitously for us, a very great friend of my old man suffered a fatal fall and his hunters had to be sold. Both had the reputation of being star performers and were to be offered at auction by Tattersalls at Knightsbridge Green with a warranty as "Good hunters, sound in eye, wind, heart, limb and action."

Alec was more than happy for us to have the two horses, provided the price was not excessive and agreed to contact the auctioneer's office to arrange the necessary credit as he could not attend the sale himself. Away we went, very excited and confident we would be the proud new owners by nightfall.

Tim was at the wheel of our big old Chrysler car known as "Pea Green", aptly named after the colour we had painted it. Towed behind was a three-horse trailer in matching livery, already set fair and with hay nets at the ready. The tool box contained brushes, head collars, night caps and bandages, just in case.

The atmosphere in the sale ring was wonderful, with old horsy characters garbed in checked knee-breeches, long rat-catcher jackets, assorted rustic waistcoats and various shapes of brown bowler. They slouched about smoking clay pipes, riding whip in hand awaiting the next lot to enter the pre-sale ring, occasionally beckoning the groom in charge to stand his charge up on his legs for inspection. Having felt the animal's limbs, peered into its eyes, curled up its lip and raised its tail for a peep up its dock, they would instruct the attendant, "Hold tight boy, I be goin' to grunt 'im." This test entailed a mighty thump with a clenched fist in the flank, whereupon the poor beast would lurch forward and the noise he made would reveal any wind impediment.

The old horsecopers would then instruct the groom to "Trot 'im up, boy!" and as the horse turned about they would draw a large spotted handkerchief from their pocket with a flourish and 'flick' the poor unsuspecting animal between the thighs. Once again the horse would jump and kick violently, the action causing him to break wind with great force, the theory being "The bigger the kick the more violent the fart" displaying a sound back. In order to carry out the same test one old dealer would place his bowler hat, green with age, on top of his walking stick and whirl it around like a Catherine wheel, making the most bizarre and frightening noise.

Seldom were these colourful gentlemen seen to bid for a horse or pony but now and then were 'dropped' a few pounds by a mug punter seeking professional advice. To digress for a moment, some forty years on when Tattersalls had moved to Newmarket, I was very taken by a big handsome grey called Birdbrook. However, I was advised not to bid by three trainer pals, Frank Cundell, Fred Winter and Fred Rimell, as they had been warned on good authority that the horse was wrong in his back. He was being ridden round the ring by a smart old lad of Sam Armstrong's, the colt's trainer. Birdbrook was very fresh, bucking and kicking with all his might while the pilot worked wonders to remain in the plate. Each time the horse let off a rip snorting fart I remembered what those old horsecopers had done some forty years before and found myself nodding for the colt by Mossborough in spite of having

11

had 'my card marked'. Once it had been knocked down to me for 1800 guineas, I said to the old fella on top: "Does this horse have a bad back?" He replied respectfully: "Could you kick and fart like that, Governor, if you had a bad back?"

Birdbrook did me proud and was as sound as a bell of brass, winning his first race over hurdles hard held by fifteen lengths. He went on to triumph on the Flat seventeen times before retiring to stud, covering his full quota of mares each season, sometimes as many as four in a day, and leaping up with such zest, the poor beast had no chance of rejecting him even if she wanted to.

Going back to the sale ring in Knightsbridge and the two hunters we hoped to purchase: the excitement was at fever pitch as the first one entered the ring. A liver chestnut with plenty of size, bone and a big bold eye, not a blood 'un but a good three parts. Bids came fast and furious from all quarters until soaring close to our limit. However, Pat and I were unaware that Alec had told Tim "not to lose either horse for the sake of a pound or two." That was good enough for her. She waved the catalogue furiously until 'Lot 140, Gallant' was knocked down to, "The charming lady with the fetching mink hat."

The tension was electric as 'Lot 141, Rompsworthy', a bright boy with black points and full of quality, entered the ring. Again the bidding was keen, with Tim nodding away like there was no tomorrow. Pat and I kept prodding her, "Go on Tim, don't lose your nerve!" When the auctioneer, with gavel poised above his head, said, "For the third and very last time," he glanced at Tim, "Come on Madam, just one more bid, you've come a long way and mustn't let your lads down." With that Tim gave a final flourish, the underbidder turned away in disgust and the auctioneer brought the hammer down without further ado. "Bravo Madam, you're a gutsy lady," he said triumphantly.

During the following months we had some super half days out hunting on Gallant and Rompworthy but boring education was spoiling our fun. Alec and Tim planned a gambling holiday at Le Touquet in France and fearful of leaving us to run riot at home alone asked our headmaster, a Bible-punching old prat, if we could leave a few days before the end of term. Permission was totally rejected, whereupon our old man flew into a rage and told the head to take a running jump or some equally meaningful expression.

After we had taken French leave our parents were informed that their twins' presence at the College would no longer be required. I went mad with joy but Pat, having the superior brain, was keen to complete his education before entering the family business. Personally, I didn't care a jot. A racehorse trainer, which I intended to become, needed the minimum of grey matter to get by.

Meanwhile, Pat got a job with the local estate agents, the boss of which was Reggie Simmonds, Master of the Berks and Bucks Stag Hounds and so he would be sure to get a bit of hunting. While my sole ambition was horsecoping — in one form or another, hopefully, I could cram in as much hunting, racing and shooting, with the odd bit of slap and tickle should the opportunity arise!

The next six months were sheer magic. I had more than my fair share of the first three sports, when out of the blue, in the early Spring of 1937, Monty Rose telephoned to ask if I would ride his daughter's mare in the members race at the Puckeridge point-to-point. Riders were restricted to members of the Hunt who had never ridden a winner under any rules. When I asked why he had been kind enough to ask me, he said that Marigold fancied me. Then hastened to correct himself by saying, "Of course, I didn't mean she fancied you personally but as a rider for her mare, Pelham Queen." I thought to myself, if I play my cards right I might have a chance with his daughter as well!

I went over to Monty's farm at Much Hadham a couple of times to school and was pleased with the way mare and owner were responding to my tender handling. We went over to Brent Pelham to walk the course the day before the race, a thrilling experience, even on foot accompanied by Marigold in her tight breeches. The next day family and entourage from Thremhall Priory turned up very early to gain pole position for their vehicles by the winning post in order to cheer me on as I went past. The members race was the very last on the card. Only three runners and my mount Pelham Queen stood out on looks, the others being decidedly coarse and hairy-heeled types with gormless pilots.

Going into the first fence in front, my mare looked like refusing so I slipped my whip through and gave her a real good back hander round the tail. Responding as if she had never been given a smack before, she grabbed hold of her bridle and proceeded to jump like a buck from then on. Over the first two or three fences I could hear the other riders swearing and blinding as they approached the obstacles but the first open ditch sorted them out. One horse cocked his jaw and ran out, crashing through the wing, while the other clouted the fence and came a frightful purler. From then on I was on my own and went past the post poised like a flat race jockey with backside cocked in the air, patting the mare on the neck as I acknowledged the roars from all my supporters.

Monty and his red-faced farmer pals were overjoyed by Marigold's success, not to mention my family who were ecstatic. As I dismounted Marigold gave me a congratulatory peck on the cheek and I though to myself 'Aye, Aye, they're off at Bogside.' Her old man, meanwhile, was busy inviting the world and his wife to

14

join him for a celebratory beverage. Having weighed in, we were ushered into the 'Hunt Farmers Only' tent, where the assembly looked as if they had been supping ale all day, some not even leaving the barrel to watch the races. The local photographer, well pissed by now, insisted Marigold get hold of her trophy with one hand and her rider with the other. Whereupon one of the young rustic yokels made a rather crude remark. To console her blushes I gave her a comforting pat on the behind.

That evening back at the farm after the mare had been set fair and rugged up for the night, Marigold asked me to help her fill a hay net up in the loft. The sloe gin was beginning to take its toll and when Marigold stumbled over a straw bale, one thing led to another and Pelham Queen had to await her reward! A great day altogether, especially when I reminded Pat that he owed me ten bob having bet that he gave me no chance with either the mare or the owner!

A while later Alec decided that a horse called Dormitory he had in training with George Digby at Newmarket, was too slow for the flat and should be flogged in the Botterill sale at Ascot. Now that I considered myself a jockey, I asked to ride the horse in a few point-to-points and maybe an amateur riders race under rules. Alec thought that was a capital idea, giving the horse a chance to mature and provide me with further experience.

I had a feeling my future was now falling into place, especially when I met a trainer called Robin Reed who agreed to take me on as a working pupil. His stables were in the village of West Ilsley below the Berkshire Downs where a number of both jumpers and flat horses were trained. My only concern was the temporary lodgings being offered to me. I had never lived away from the comforts of home as my parents disliked boarding school, hence we were educated in Bishops

Stortford College as day boys. I was to share a large double bed up in the attic of the trainer's rambling old Georgian mansion and my meals would be provided by a Mrs Betty Pushover at her cottage down the far end of the village.

When I cast up at the yard Robin Reed explained that Paddy O'Leary, an Irish jockey, had come over to ride one of the stables' novice chasers at Stratford the next day. Robin told me he would introduce me to my room mate when he got back from the phone box. At that moment there was an agonised scream from outside the stable gate. We all rushed out to see what the commotion was and there was poor Paddy with a bicycle wedged between his legs. Apparently a small apprentice perched on a large bicycle without any brakes, had come tearing round the corner on the wrong side of the road and crashed straight into Paddy's groin.

Clutching his private parts he groaned in excruciating pain. A doctor was called who insisted Paddy should be sent to hospital. I thought that at least I would have the bed to myself that night.

Finally I strode along to Mrs Pushover for a quick bit of breakfast. Although I knew the lady had strict rules about times for meals, I assumed she would make an exception under the bizarre circumstances. I tapped on the door, prepared to be ultra polite and the window was flung open upstairs revealing the head of the ugliest female I had ever clapped eyes on. A big coarse face of sallow complexion, protruding yellow teeth, scraggy black hair, in desperate need of a wash, and copious warts not enhancing the revolting ensemble. I hurriedly tried to explain the position but before slamming the window she roared, "If you think I'm goin' to cook you an effing breakfast at this time of the day, you've got another effing think coming.'

16

Now totally disillusioned by my initial introduction to the racing scene I started to slouch off back to the yard. On the way I passed the one and only shop, a small post office, and in the window was a notice on a bit of cardboard offering 'Home made candy within.' Starving hungry I decided to pop in and buy a bag to eat on the way back. The bell clanged loudly as I pushed open the door and there on the counter, displayed on a glass cake stand, was a large block of coconut ice. White, pink, brown and green. I asked the post mistress, an ancient old biddy, if I could have a taste of the icing. She sliced off a sliver and awaited my verdict: "Delicious, and the green portion adds a delicate flavour of mint. I'll take the lot if I may."

By the time I reached the yard, half the block of icing had gone and the lads hanging around in the tack room very soon devoured the remainder.

I decided I could not stand the living arrangements any longer, as the thought of my bed-mate and breakfast arrangements at Betty Pushover's gave me the creeps. The lads recommended I should try for a 'pad' at the Horse & Jockey, a small pub in the nearby village of Chilton, and added in typical language that 'the bit behind the bar was a rare sort with tits sticking out like organ stops and buttocks that left you well.'

I was very soon on my bike and pedalling away over the hill across the downs and, sure enough, when following the shapely wench up two flights of stairs to be shown a small single room at the top, I could see what the lads meant!

Life for the next few months was great, both at the Horse & Jockey and at the stable yard. The girl behind the bar turned out to be the daughter of a trainer who had stables in the village of Chilton. We became more than good friends and spent many an afternoon up on the gallops just listening to the skylarks! I was riding plenty of work and learning the tricks of the trade in the

17

racing game, in fact my life was progressing according to plan. My elder brother Peter introduced me to a stunning-looking girl he had taken out a time or two in London. Her name was Kay Long and I knew instantly that this was love at first sight, the one and only for me, not just for a bit of slap and tickle but for always no matter what. Hard to imagine, but apparently she had the same feelings and after an exciting courtship in and around Dolphin Square Swimming Baths in London, as Kay was a high-board diver of Olympic standard, we took the plunge and church bells chimed. Sixty years this November, we are still together, not doing much diving mind, but very happy and with few regrets.

Kay Long training for the Olympic Games. (I am not the anchorman!)

I digress. Reverting to West Ilsley, I persuaded Robin Reed to allow me to enter Dormitory in a selling

18

hurdle for amateur riders at Gatwick, but to cut a long story shorter I fell foul of the racecourse stewards even before I had climbed aboard in the paddock. I was fined for pre-race misdemeanours, a term which the press used freely the following day in The Sporting Life. Shamed and being an honourable gentleman, my old man sued the Jockey Club Stewards for libel on behalf of his then 'infant' son.

The mammoth hearing was held in the High Court before Lord Chief Justice Lord Hewart, with leading lawyers Gilbert Beyfus KC acting on our behalf and Norman Birkett KC for the defendants. The battle raged fast and furious for three hectic days at enormous costs to both sides. Finally justice prevailed with a total win for the plaintiff. Damages and full costs were awarded against the Jockey Club and the racing journalists made much of the fact that never before in the history of this illustrious body had they lost a case in a court of law.

RACEHORSE OWNER'S SON GETS £200 FOR LIBEL

Michael Pope.

TWO hundred pounds damages with costs were awarded Mr. Michael Brownfield Pope, amateur rider, of The Barn House, Cherry Gardens-lane, Maidenhead, to-day.

It was the third day of the case, in which he was suing racecourse stewards and a clerk of the course for libel before the Lord Chief Justice (Lord Hewart), sitting with a special jury in the King's Bench Division.

The defendants were Mr. Ernest E. Robinson, Clerk of the Course at Gatwick Race Meeting on February 3, 1938, and Commander A. V. Courage, Baron Francis de Tuyll and Mr. T. H. Lloyd, acting stewards at the same meeting.

SUED THROUGH FATHER

They were sued for damages by

Chapter Three

CALL TO ARMS

When it was announced in September 1939 that we were at war with Germany my brother Peter and I strode off to Knightsbridge Barracks full of up and at 'em spirit and determined to joint the Household Cavalry, the last of the mounted regiments in the country to survive mechanisation.

Ever since I was a child I had but one ambition – to become involved with horses as a career and for recreational purposes. If I was to defend my King and Country then it had to be astride a charger, not from a tank, aircraft, ship or on my flat feet.

Imagine my disappointment, therefore, when I was blandly informed that Peter had passed his medical but I had failed, being half an inch too short. While I disputed the fact vigorously, the medical officer hastened to explain that the measurement discrepancy concerned my height and not the length of my courting tackle!

The orderly handling the measuring stick suggested I pop across the parade ground to the cobbler's shop where his pal 'Nobby the Snob' would be sure to attach false heels to my shoes if I dropped him a sweetener. Sure enough, a backhander all round and I'd gone up in the world sufficiently for Pope brothers to be signed on as troopers in the Royal Horse Guards.

We could have opted to join the Life Guards but the word 'horse' included in the title of the former regiment swayed our decision. Expecting to go directly into the riding school mounted on a sleek black charger we were somewhat disillusioned at being marched straight onto the barracks square in our civilian clothes, to be addressed by an enormous great red-faced Regimental Sergeant Major.

Troopers Michael and Peter Pope in uniform.

He was a very loud, coarse, rude and offensive brute who obviously took an immediate dislike to me and my 'rat catching' attire. He roared like a bull. "To the barber's shop at the double for a short back and sides you dozy-looking pouf, then down into the town for a good strong woman to make a man of you. There is no shortage of tarts hanging around the castle walls who have better things for breakfast." I thought to myself, if this is the disgraceful sort of behaviour one encounters in the Royal Family's own regiment, responsible for guarding our King and Country, I feel his Majesty should be told about it. I made a mental note to have a word with the Duke of Beaufort, our troop leader, as I felt certain he would not condone such shameful and uncouth behaviour.

I must admit that I did obey the order to get my hair cut, albeit only a light trim by a stylish barber in the town, rather than have it shaved off like a convict at the regimental sheep shearers. However, I totally disobeyed the order to indulge in sexual intercourse up against the castle wall in broad daylight.

Very soon we were allotted an old horse apiece, hardly the gleaming black chargers we had visualised galloping into action at a furious pace. In fact, my conveyance, B 37, could hardly shuffle along and was obviously plagued with painful corns. I reported the matter to the farrier who replied in typical trooper language, "Give 'im a prod in the ribs with 'yer spurs and 'e'll figet 'e ever 'ad any effing feet."

Before very long brother Peter was promoted to Corporal in charge of our troop, the Duke of Beaufort having considered he had shown initiative by wearing string gloves, laundered daily, to pick up his horse's droppings rather than using bare hands, the customary method for mucking out in the Household Cavalry.

Our troop was highly honoured to be given the task of guarding the Royal Family when in residence at the Royal Lodge in Windsor Park. Our Headquarters were at the foot of the Copper Horse, a famous landmark within the park, whence we patrolled in pairs on our poor old screws throughout the night with swords drawn, in case of attack by enemy parachutists.

Should such an invasion take place we had orders to use our own initiative as to how we handled the situation, the officers in charge, mainly peacetime soldiers, already considered the operation beneath their dignity and treated it as a cosmetic exercise. Personally, I took the matter very seriously and planned to allow the invaders to float down from the skies to within an arms length and then thrust the point of my sabre up their backsides with all my might, while chanting our troop's somewhat risqué war cry, ending "How's that for centre?"

...should an invasion take place we had orders to use our own initiative.

Sadly, before being given the opportunity to test my strategy, it was announced that all our horses were to be withdrawn and replaced by infernal machines. Naturally, we were devastated. Our ambition to take part in a cavalry charge had been thwarted. Just as well, no doubt, in view of the fact that our steeds were too old and infirm to raise a decent canter, let alone a gallop and would be facing machine guns rather than bows and arrows.

Chapter Four

Having been grounded we were given the opportunity to become commissioned officers. Much to our disgust Peter and I were sent off to different Cadet units, but thanks to Colonel David Dawnay, Commanding Officer of a regiment called the North Irish Horse, we found ourselves re-united as officers in a cavalry outfit—now equipped with Churchill tanks. In spite of being horseless the Colonel still preferred to enlist subalterns with horsy backgrounds.

Months passed as we strove to become accustomed to our ghastly new weapons, noisy, greasy, smelly and terribly uncomfortable great hulks of steel. Eventually, orders came through confirming that we were to be sent overseas to take part in the North Africa campaign. After an uneventful voyage on the S.S. Duchess of York, we steamed into Algiers harbour.

The sun shone brightly, glamorising a patchwork scene of pink, white and blue buildings faded by time, the glare of the sun and poverty. In fantasy, we could have been about to enjoy the pleasures of a dreamy winter holiday, but in reality we were about to be introduced to the horrors of war.

We had expected to be reunited with our tanks and transport once ashore. Instead, we were told that through unforeseen circumstances our vehicles had been sent up the coast to Philippeville and we would have to march out of town to a transit camp for the night. The first few miles tramping over cobblestones through the streets of Algiers were sheer hell and by the time we arrived at our destination we were moving like a bevy of old tarts in tight high heels. More painfully, it had played merry hell with my dormant haemorrhoids.

Despite a powerful beverage on arrival at the Camp, a pal of mine performed a miracle and produced an outsize bottle of Gordons full strength gin from the NAAFI. As we sat with our poor feet soaking in buckets of cold water in a nearby grove, we plucked the fruit from the trees to dilute the mothers ruin with the juice from the blood oranges. Draining the bottle between us we collapsed into a drunken stupor, not caring if it snowed bricks. The next morning, while having our feet attended to by a medical orderly, we were told we could write home to assure our families we had arrived safely. I declined the offer, visualising my family tearfully awaiting the postman to pedal over the hill on his bog wheel with news of our first blood-thirsty clash with the enemy. I didn't have the guts to tell them the true facts. Our tanks had gone missing, there wasn't a hostile German in sight and my only injuries were red raw feet, palpitating piles and a hangover!

The following morning we were herded like cattle into a small naval vessel, the crew of which warned us to be prepared for attack by one-man submarines. Officers with pistols and other ranks with rifles were the only weapons we had to defend ourselves with and as we lined the decks the sight was just too much for the sailors. They burst out laughing before admitting they had been 'taking the piss.'

We finally reach Philippeville after an uneventful voyage, only to find that panic reigned. Our Colonel, David Dawnay, had just returned from the front where 'A' Squadron of our regiment was already occupying a holding position. He reported that the situation was very grave as the Germans were preparing to launch a major offensive. We were ordered to unload our tanks from the ship as fast as we could, then drive them straight on to the road transporters for an immediate dash through the night to Le Keffe. On arrival we would receive further orders.

25

It appeared to be me that our regiment was scattered far and wide across the country, some of the tanks already at the front, some on rail and others on transporters. Apparently, they had been shipped to three different ports; Boujie, Algiers and Philippeville, either by mistake or design. We knew not which, but only hoped that someone did. I was sorely tempted to ask a few questions, but thought it best to follow the advice of the Regimental Corporal Major Poupart of the Royal Horse Guards, who proclaimed: "If you want to succeed as a soldier, keep your mouth shut, your bowels open and never ever volunteer for anything."

What a journey. We travelled right through the night, perched up on our tanks, loaded onto road transporters, weighing a total of close on 80 tons. It was pouring with rain, pitch black and the surface of the winding, hilly road was like glass. Soaked to the skin, freezing cold and starving hungry, we eventually cast up at Le Keff. Hats off to the drivers of the transporters. They were fantastic, handling their vehicles like dodgem cars on the steep mountain roads in total darkness at break-neck speed.

Two troops of 'B' Squadron, including my own No. 4 Troop, were given orders to head for Beja on their own tracks with all speed and be prepared to go straight into action. Another horrific journey which seemed to take forever, with fuel running dangerously low, the petrol tankers having been diverted by the Military Police for some unseen reason. Eventually, we clattered into Beja just before dawn, thinking we would be sure of a brief respite to change our soaked clothing and get some grub inside us. No such luck. Everyone was in a frightful flap when our Squadron Leader, Major John Rew, arrived effing and blinding, having been hunting down the missing petrol tankers.

Horseless: the Churchill tank—the conveyance for our cavalry regiment, the North Irish Horse.

He warned us that there was a major crisis and we must press on with all speed once we had refuelled. After some discussion as to who should lead the column of six tanks, I foolishly volunteered, scorning the wisdom of Regimental Corporal Major Poupart. The instructions were to proceed straight along the main road until spotting a guide in an armoured scout car on the left hand side. The driver would confirm our orders, unless there had been a change, that three tanks were to fan out on either side of the road and take up hull-down positions under the ridge ahead. The road was straight but rolled on and on, up and down over bleak country. One ridge after another with barely a landmark on the map to guide us. I kept thinking as each ridge loomed up, what if our guide has got lost or been bumped off, we could well go roaring straight up over the hill into the jaws of the enemy and land up in the bag without firing a round in anger. I began to appreciate Poupart's sound advise not to volunteer for anything!

On again over yet another rise, even bleaker with neither hair nor hide of man or beast. Suddenly, I spotted a lone figure on foot walking towards us dragging what looked like a small goat or dog. After a quick look through my binoculars I got on to the radio to report this odd sighting. John Rew said it was probably an old Arab but to take no changes as it could just be a spy in disguise to suss out our strength. If in any doubt, give him a barrel, there were plenty more where he came from!

As the crumpled figure got closer it was clearly an old woman draped in black clothes hobbling on a stick with a scruffy little dog in tow. As the old girl reached the tank I could see she was very, very old and likely as daft as a bat. Feeling sorry for the poor biddy I tossed her a tin of bully beef, and with a toothless grin she mumbled, 'Danke Schön, Fritz.' As she shuffled slowly away I thought, no doubt she already has a tin of German liverwurst and a couple of Sauerkraut stuffed up her 'Unterhosen'.

Moving forward very slowly over the next brow, we suddenly spotted our guide at the side of the road waving his beret furiously while flashing a signal lamp. Wasting no time he repeated the orders: "Three tanks to the left of the road and three to the right. Then move forward to take up a hull-down position under the crest of the hill. You are to cover the right flank and 'A' Squadron is already in position to your left. Tell your crews to stay in their tanks, as the enemy captured the highest observation point in the area last night and can now see every move we make."

As we crawled forward into position I felt an urgent need to relieve nature. The moment we halted I hopped out of the turret. Even before I had time to drop my trousers a mortar landed with a hell of a crack dangerously close. Scrambling back into the tank I immediately gave orders to all crews that ablutions, no matter how urgent, would have to wait until after dark. I then radioed John Rew to report that we were in position. He sounded less cheerful than usual. "

"You'll be sorry to hear that both Dick Hern and Bill Ketchells have been wounded and evacuated, but hopefully they will be back to fight another day," he said.

Having been standing up in the tank for what seemed like days on end with only brief spells of relief, my feet and ankles were now throbbing madly. As I kicked off my boots I could see that my legs were starting to swell.

At dusk our artillery opened up with their heavy guns, concentrating on the enemy tank position with one helluva force. This allowed us the opportunity to get out and attend to our overdue toiletry and even chance a good brew up. The deafening barrage went on throughout the night with barely a break. At dawn a radio report came through, telling us the German tanks had been destroyed, badly damaged or abandoned. In fact, the enemy had taken a frightful thrashing.

By now my poor old legs were the size of tree trunks and fit to explode. My crew quite rightly encouraged me to hand over command of the troop to my sergeant, then draw my tank back some fifty yards while arrangements were made for the medical team to pick me up in their armoured vehicle and take me back for treatment at the tented field hospital.

I hadn't even got to the hospital before the news came through that John Rew had been killed by a mortar shell while leaning out of his tank. A terrible shock for all his friends and for the Regiment. He was a grand person, a brave soldier and always cheerful. I remember so well attending his wedding not long before we came abroad, when he wed a girl nick-named Zulu. It was such a happy affair with many of his colleagues from the North Irish Horse seeing them off

29

in style. Zulu was not only an attractive girl but a seriously stylish horsewoman.

On arrival at the tented hospital, chock-a-block with members of all ranks suffering varying complaints and injuries, the staff appeared to be in a state of flux. The nurse hurriedly examined my legs with the toes now spread out like a bunch of bananas, or rather well hung beef, turning the colour of mahogany. She told me that a very important visitor, accompanied by a general from the War Office, was expected at any time to survey the battle conditions at the front. I enquired if she knew who the VIP was. "Oh! It's Churchill," said the nurse.

Christ! I thought, how foolhardy to allow the great man himself so close to the sharp end when the outcome of the entire war is virtually in his hands. My look of surprise must have caused the girl to add, "I don't mean Winston Churchill. It's his son Randolph." I had now lost interest in the inspection and was much more concerned about my poor old legs. A young doctor then appeared and assumed me that if I kept my feet up for two or three days, with some pills to thin the blood, I would soon be back at the front fit to fight. A while later a fellow on a stretcher was dumped onto the bed alongside me. The poor chap looked desperately ill, as if about to throw in the towel. Apparently he was a pilot who had baled out over enemy lines some ten days previously and while in hiding developed malaria and jaundice. Nearly an hour later he was still lying fully clothed with his boots on, so I signalled to a fierce looking Matron as she stomped past with bed pan at the ready. "This airman is in a very bad way and needs urgent attention." She mumbled something about being very busy but did at least come across to look at the poor devil. Pulling the blanket up over his head she turned to me and said, "You have no need to worry about him any longer, he's a goner."

I thought to myself, "Poor bugger, what a way to go after all you have been through." But, to be fair, the doctor who had attended him obviously knew there was no chance of recovery and had hopefully slipped him a farewell potion to help him on his way.

Lying flat on my back with my feet stuck up in the air I must have dozed off, only to be awakened by the sound of loud voices at the foot of my bed. Opening one eye, I could see an enormously tall General with a bristling moustache, covered in medals, crowns, pips, stars and gold braid. Alongside him was a fellow who had to be Randolph Churchill with a face of pugnacious bulldog features, resembling his illustrious father, even without the customary Havana cigar. In a loud voice, ignoring me as if I were unconscious, Randolph said, "And what ails this fellow?" The doctor accompanying the party on their tour of inspection said, "He was brought in from the front this morning with phlebitis, having been forced to stand in his tank on and off for over forty-eight hours." Randolph retorted, obviously having been instructed to take an intelligent interest, "Well why did he not get out of his tank and lie underneath it for a spell?" Just as I was about to give him both barrels, the old brass hat, who I learned later had been a very big noise in the First World War, intervened, relieving me of the honour of answering such a fatuous remark. "Those with any experience of tank warfare would know full well that such action under shell fire would be suicidal."

As if anxious to make amends for his ignorant comment, Randolph changed the subject rapidly: "General, I don't wish to embarrass you in front of the ladies but your fly buttons are undone." The old boy guffawed as he fumbled to adjust his address, then said, "How diligent of you Randolph. However, your observation is immaterial as a dead bird seldom falls out of its nest!"

With truce declared and dignitaries settling for a draw they moved on. A little corporal of the Argylls had taken the place of the airman, who by now had been carted off on a trolley to the mortuary, and the doctor appeared eager to bypass his replacement. However, the General, not accustomed to being hoodwinked snapped, "And what, may I ask, is wrong with this chappie?" The doctor replied, "Only a minor complaint General, he had an abdominal infection. As quick as lightning the General barked, "You mean he has a dose of the clap." Then he turned on the poor little man, now out of bed and standing to attention, "If you must muck about with women of ill-repute why the hell don't you use the Army issue contraceptives, intercourse for the use of." The corporal, looking rather overcome, replied, "Och! I canna abide those rubber things. It's like going to bed with yer socks on."

My next visitor was a fellow officer in our regiment called Dick Bowring who had popped in to see how I was getting on. When he heard about my previous distinguished bedside callers he told me that Randolph Churchill was to be attached to our regiment for a short period in order to gain experience of tank action under battle conditions in the front line. Some weeks later I learned how lucky I had been not to be selected as his tutor, as either through extreme bravery, bravado, or stupidity he had urged his troop leader to take the most daring and alarming tactical chances scaring merry hell out of all and sundry. By this over zealous action he had no doubt hoped to emulate the courage and fighting spirit of his old man. However, by the time he had departed for another sector of the front, apart from leaving a trail of somewhat shattered nerves, he had become liked and respected by officers and other ranks alike.

With feet still stuck up in the air I had time to reflect on my thoughts of the War and my experiences to date. To me everything appeared so confused, chaotic and lacking in both planning and information. But since I was only a very junior officer I decided it would be wise to heed the first of old Poupart's golden rules and keep my mouth shut. So far there had been precious little chance to carry out the second theory which concerned one's motions, and foolishly to my cost I had ignored the third.

I had now returned to my troop, who were preparing to advance northwards, the sting having been temporarily taken out of the enemy. Our orders were somewhat undefined, but rumour had it that we must prepare for a major offensive. In an attempt to keep fully abreast of the battle in our immediate sector I stayed glued to the radio, listening to orders and information passing between our Squadron Leader and the troops under his command. Even then there were times when I had to miss out, as my radio operator would request permission to switch over to the National Forces programme from London so that all sets would be netted into Vera Lynn singing either 'The White Cliffs of Dover', 'We'll Meet Again' or 'Yours Till the End of Life's Story'. Troops everywhere, young and old, would virtually ignore the battle in progress to listen to 'our' Vera. With tears in their eyes they would dream of dear old mum, the missus, the fiancée, or bit on the side back home.

I decided that this practice must cease, but was sharply reminded that the Germans were given a similar dispensation. I was assured that they listened to Marlene Dietrich with her renderings of 'Falling in Love Again', 'Lili Marlene' and 'The Boys in the Back Room?'. No doubt these ladies had a beneficial effect on the morale of the troops on both sides, but at times I could willingly have throttled the pair of them. I never did find out if the timings of the broadcasts were synchronised, thus creating a temporary truce and cease-fire.

Chapter Five

THE BATTLE FOR LONGSTOP HILL

Tank crews and infantry liaise at first light.

As it turned out that major offensive, after a few minor skirmishes en route, was to be almost certainly the most important of the North African campaign. Longstop Hill consisted of a long range of rugged hills climbing gradually before rising almost vertically to a massive peak known as Djebel Rhar, the last bastion before the heights fall away to Teboura and Tunis beyond.

The battle raged furiously on and off for five days and our regiment played many roles in support of the infantry forces. However, it was not until the final phase that my own personal troop of Churchill tanks was thrown into the fray and, naturally, that is the operation I can best recall.

On the evening of the fourth day I was crouched under the backside of a tank playing poker with my crew when a dispatch rider came roaring out of the gloaming enquiring as to the whereabouts of a certain Lieutenant Michael Brownfield Pope. Brownfield does happen to be my middle name, although I have never used it—not being hyphenated. So why the hell staff at headquarters had dug it out of the files at such a bizarre moment I'll never know. The message he carried came from Colonel David Dawnay, our commanding officer. It read: "Please report to my caravan immediately. Extremely important. Signed David Dawnay."

No only was he a first class and highly respected soldier, but a great character and good friend, especially to the 'horsy' members of the regiment such as Dick Hern, myself and a few other 'donkey wallopers'. David was, in fact, a celebrated horseman both on the polo field and in the hunting field and after the war was appointed by the Queen to control Ascot as Clerk of the Course.

Hitching a ride: infantry get a lift to the front.

I grabbed a map and leapt onto the back of the messenger's motorbike. On arriving at the caravan, with walls plastered with maps smothered in flags and coloured drawing pins, I was introduced to the Colonel of the Buffs. He had only assumed command the day before as sadly his predecessor had been killed earlier in the battle.

Looking slightly harassed and short of sleep, David said, "Mike, the regiment has been chosen to support the Buffs in the final attack of Longstop Hill. As you know, the two highest peaks, Djebel Ahmera and Djebel Rhar, are still in enemy hands. Although reconnaissance patrols report that all approaches, especially to the latter, are considered too steep for tanks to handle, and without close armoured support, it presents a nigh on impossible task for the infantry.

"General Alexander, nevertheless, has issued the Brigadier with a direct order. 'Attack and destroy enemy forces on Djebel Rhar at all costs.' I have subsequently ordered 'B' Squadron to support the Buffs and carry out the attack. Although it's a tough task, it will be an enormous honour if the North Irish Horse can help achieve such an important victory.

David continued: "Djebel Rhar is the king-pin of the whole operation. It is such a restricted and narrow front up the final slopes only one troop of tanks can be usefully employed to support the infantry. Gordon Russell, your Squadron Leader has nominated No. 4 Troop to carry out the role and that is why I'm especially anxious to have a chat with you personally, being the Troop Leader, before you are briefed."

From past experience I'd learned that seldom was it a mistake to grovel to senior officers and duly said how privileged I was that my troop had been given the task, while at the time thinking to myself, 'That jolly old General Alexander must think we are a bunch of half-witted mountain goats.'

David went on: "In view of the importance of the operation the Brigadier and I intend to control the operation personally. Our vehicle will be in direct wireless communication with your tank and any support you may need on the ground, or from the air, will be made available. It's your show and we will not interfere unless it's absolutely necessary." Scratching his bum — this was one of the Colonel's characteristics — he said, "Mike, we are counting on you and your troop to succeed."

The deafening artillery barrage continued throughout the night with unrelenting ferocity, followed by horrendous strafing by aircraft at first light. I remember thinking, with my head under a blanket and cotton wool stuffed into my earholes, how can any poor bastard survive such an onslaught? And, if compelled to remain in a cramped dug-out on the hillside, how does one relieve nature? Surely, to do it on your own doorstep, as you might say, must be hell for one's morale and equally offensive for one's comrades!

We didn't have long to wait on the starting line before an authoritative voice cracked over the air on the dot of 08.30: "Hello Roger 4, Sunray here, confirm you are receiving me strength nine and are prepared to advance." I replied: "Hello Sunray. Am receiving you loud and clear and am rarin' to go, Roger and out," purposely trying to sound enthusiastic and keen (although trembling like a jelly) to inspire my crew and instil some personal confidence.

Whilst giving the order to advance, I gave a quick glance at the pictures pinned up in the turret of the tank — my wife Kay, who was due to foal down any day, and Shaun, my son, barely two years old. This may sound a sloppy and sentimental thing to do but I can assure you I was not the only one to pay his respects to family and loved ones before embarking on such a potentially dicey operation for fear it might be the last.

It had been planned that the infantry, from now on referred to as 'markers' for purposes of radio security, should proceed along the upper slopes, with the tanks pursuing a parallel course on the lower approaches leading up the foothills of Djebel Ahmera and Djebel Rhar. We had gone only a short distance, following a route which had been cleared of mines right through from the start line to a reasonable distance beyond, when there was an almighty bang. After the dust had settled it was clear that one of my tank tracks had been blown off.

Map of Tunisia showing in detail our theatre of war.

Paddy, my driver, an Irish stable lad in peacetime, and never short of an appropriate quip, shouted up the intercom, "That's buggered it boss, the old cow's spread a plate!" Having checked we were all in one piece I called up my Corporal's tank and told him to draw

38

upsides, then I hopped across and changed places—a real huntsman's change of horses if ever there was. Surprisingly, he and my crew were far from chuffed at missing the scrap. Although I assured them they could catch up once repairs had been completed, I was kidding myself that the mere sight of tanks would give the Germans such a bloody awful shock they might well be grovelling for mercy by mid-day.

Proceeding slowly through the lines of a cleared minefield.

I told my new driver to give our charger a kick in the ribs and we soon caught up with the foot sloggers to our right and left. I remember reminiscing that they looked rather like a line of guns and beaters walking up grouse on a moor in Scotland on the Glorious Twelfth. A sudden rattle of enemy machine gun fire soon made me concentrate on the job in hand. Luckily, my Sergeant, Ted O'Hare had spotted a flash. A short burst from his Bessa instantly settled that argument.

The battle was now hotting up and the Buffs were being given a terrible pounding from accurate shelling and airbursts, which pinned them down under a dense cloud of dust. Thankfully, the offending weapons were no match for those of our Churchill tanks and between us we proceeded to knock seven bells out of a mortar and four machine gun posts. The infantry boys soon appeared out of the dust and pressed on with amazing bravery and spirit.

Their Colonel came running across and scrambled up the back of my tank to talk to me through the hatch in the turret, and although I warned him that he was a sitting target he didn't appear the least bit concerned. We made a quick assessment of the situation and agreed that the best chance of our capturing the awesome looking objective was for the tanks to charge up the hill with all possible speed making as much noise as possible in the hope of frightening the living daylights out of the Krauts.

He agreed to follow on with his fellows as fast and as close as he could, mopping up any prisoners we might put in the bag as we advanced. After we had wished each other good luck I told my Sergeant to attack the southern slope of the hill whilst I would attempt the western side and hopefully we would marry up at the top.

To start with the going wasn't too bad but it became increasingly difficult—rough, extremely steep, flaming hot and very dusty. On manoeuvring around a large cluster of rock, I suddenly spotted the muzzle of a 75mm, anti-tank gun only a few yards ahead. I yelled at my gunner, "Anti tank gun twelve o'clock, give it hell." A round of 6-pounder and a burst of Bessa brought two pairs of hands frantically waving from a hole in the ground behind the gun.

It was extremely encouraging to note the ghastly state of the prisoners as they crawled out of a hole like drowned rats, tired, hungry, unshaven and clearly longing to quit the War—so different from the arrogant bastards we had encountered in earlier scraps. I asked them in sign language if there were any more anti-tank guns ahead of us and the answer was 'nein, nein' which was certainly reassuring news indeed.

Pressing on once again I called up my Sergeant on the radio to find out how he was progressing. "We're going great guns and have taken a bundle of prisoners with very little opposition," he said. "I have disarmed the poor bastards and sent them shuffling down the hill. But we are temporarily held up as my driver has had to get out to put some oil in the tank's engine. He says the pressure reads 'danger' and she'll blow up if we don't give her a drink."

A tank crew repairs tracks in haste under fire.

By now I was confident that the Germans were at breaking point and ready to quit. If we made enough noise they might even decide to capitulate. On the other hand, if they woke up to the fact that our armoured

41

force consisted of only two tanks they might well find renewed courage and have a go at us.

Dropping down into bottom gear and grinding up higher and higher, as we edged around a blind corner we suddenly encountered an amazing sight I'm certain none of us will ever forget. There, about 30 yards straight ahead, was a sheer cliff face with twenty or more Germans crammed together, arms above their heads waving anything white they could get their hands on and shouting 'Aufgeben, Aufgeben' pathetically pleading for mercy.

Who could blame the poor devils for capitulating when confronted by a thirty ton caterpillar-like monster, bristling with menacing weapons against which they had little or no defence—firstly alarmed by the great roar of the engines, then terrified to see the massive beasts appear from behind a rock threatening extermination.

The steepness of the climb and the unlikely prospect of our ever reaching the top of the hill meant we were somewhat disorientated. At that very moment the Buffs Colonel scrambled onto the back of my tank once more, just in time to hear my Sergeant's wildly excited voice shouting, "We've made it, we're right on top of the Djebel Rhar." Sure enough, there we were, surrounded by hordes of scruffy-looking German soldiers all begging for mercy and throwing their arms to the ground like some ancient conquered tribe."

What a wonderfully exhilarating moment for all concerned to realise that the battle had been won without suffering major casualties, apart from the pride of the five unfortunate fellows we left behind listening in on the wireless while struggling to repair our disabled tank.

David Dawnay could restrain himself no long and, bursting with pride, roared over the air, "Wonderful news, Mike. We will be coming forward immediately to greet you. Please convey our congratulations to Marker Sunray and all you chaps, meanwhile."

Already acclaimed as a glorious victory it should be remembered that our task had been made one hell of a sight easier by our forces who had both weakened the defences and demoralised the enemy in earlier battles leading up to the grand finale. It was the incredibly courageous infantry who had taken such a ghastly hammering.

They were the boys who should receive the honour and the glory for the overall victory of the Battle for Longstop Hill and I for one salute them with the utmost sincerity. But for their bravery many of us engaged in the final operation would have undoubtedly perished. Nevertheless, I suppose someone had to get lucky and deliver the far less dangerous but much more opportune, coup de grace.

It wasn't long before the rabble or dishevelled prisoners came shuffling down the dusty track, escorted by a party of Buffs with our tanks whipping in. On reaching the lower ground we spotted what appeared to be three scout cars approaching from the distance in clouds of dust, dispersing into the air a cumulus of sheep shit and shingles.

The reception we received from David and all the other brasshats, who had joined the bandwagon, was almost embarrassing. I tried to explain that it was not solely our efforts that had won the day. When the enemy realised that the tanks were handling the country, resistance had weakened rapidly and finally collapsed altogether.

However, none of the welcoming party appeared to be remotely interested in my theory and who was I to minimise the thrill and glory of such a magnificent victory. Some of them were no doubt visualising promotion let alone the odd medal as well. A few days later in the prisoner of war cage a very high-ranking

German officer responsible for the entire defences of Longstop Hill explained with surprising humility: "The Djebel Rhar was considered to be the strongest outpost of the Western defence and I was prepared to hold it against a full scale attack by the best British infantry forces. But when it was apparent that Churchill tanks were capable of handling the terrain so well I knew that the battle was lost and the defence line in front of Tunis would be broken."

Just as we were preparing to push on back to base, the German officer who had been in charge of the Djebel Rhar itself broke rank from the prisoners' column and strode across towards David Dawnay. Saluting in a most arrogant, almost theatrical manner, he roared defiantly: "I am the Commander of the German Grenadier Regiment and my officers are entitled to transport under the Geneva Convention."

I have never seen David Dawnay so rattled or angry as he pulled his revolver, stuck it into the German's ribs and retorted: "I don't give a damn if you are a bloody lance corporal in the Catering Corps, get back into the ranks at once or I'll shoot you."

David drew his leg back as far as he could and, red-faced with fury, booted the arrogant pig up the backside. Being the blue-eyed boy of the moment I thought there was no harm in mentioning that a decent looking pair of binoculars were hanging around the fellow's neck! David replied, "Go help yourself Mike and don't stand any nonsense from that aggressive swine."

Completely knackered and drained of all feeling, with sand and dust in every orifice of man and machine, we crawled back to base dreaming of a long hot soak in a large deep bath, followed by lashings of ice cold champagne, both of which were, of course, only wishful thinking.

The best we could hope for was a dip in the murky water of the river Meduarda, followed by a few cans of tepid NAAFI beer if we were lucky.

These inhuman conditions reminded me of a story I heard of an effeminate young man pitched into the forces straight from Eton, who wrote home to his mother after his very first experience in the battlefield.

"Mumsie darling, I was made to fight today and it was too, too frightening for words. My dear, the noise, the smell, the dust, the language, the blood and oh! the people, all so coarse and common, it was simply shattering. Conditions back at camp are equally barbaric, even the lavatory paper is rationed and one is forced to use the Picture Post. All so uncomfortable and unsatisfactory, especially as there is no bidet available.

"In the hope of hastening promotion and therefore enjoying better conditions, I spoke to our Colonel as you suggested Mumsie darling, letting it slip that uncle was a very senior Brigadier in the Artillery. He merely laughed and said, 'Funny fellas those gunnahs, fart at meals times and call each other buggahs.' Please, please Mumsie darling get uncle to have me transferred to the War Office in Whitehall."

That evening, while listening to the day's experiences of my blokes, before compiling a battle report, I asked my sergeant's driver what he would have done if he had been attacked while putting oil in his engine. He replied: "I would have thrown the bloody oil can at the bastard and then shot him in the balls with my revolver." No need to tell you he was an Irishman!"

Shortly afterwards he, together with a number of officers and other ranks, were duly recommended for medals. The news that I had been mentioned for a

Military Cross[1] naturally filled me with pride but it bothered me. Had I truly earned such an honour? I imagined many others felt equally unworthy of their various awards. The excitement of the glorious event soon died down. However, it had enhanced my reputation for 'being born with a golden horseshoe up my backside.' A few days later I received a cable to say that my wife, Kay, was in great heart and had duly delivered a healthy colt foal. Believe it or not, shortly afterwards I was told that I would be returning home by air to lecture green young subalterns, already trained and due to be posted abroad for active service, in the art of tank warfare under battle conditions. What is more the Training School turned out to be at Oriel College, Oxford, only a few miles from my home.

---

[1] See Appendix 1, page 90, a facsimile of Michael Pope's MC citation, which read as follows: 'On 26 Apr Lieut. M. B. Pope commanded the fwd right tp of 'B' Sqn in the final assault on the Djebel Rhar. During the course of this successful action which finally placed Long Stop in our hands, Lieut Pope's troop silenced seven MGs and captured an 88mm A/Tk gun intact after engaging it from the flank. Over 50 prisoners surrendered to his troop and these he shepherded along for a considerable time before handing them over to the Inf. Throughout this engagement Lieut. Brownfield Pope displayed great initiative and resource. He handled his troop with coolness, daring and judgement and his support of the Inf was magnificent. He also displayed great courage when changing tks under MG fire and his conduct was an example and inspiration to his troop. [D. Dawnay, Lieut.-Colonel, Commanding North Irish Horse; dated Field, 27 Apr 43.]

46

Back home on leave with Kay and old friends.

When I returned overseas some weeks later the North Irish Horse had moved to Algeria, harboured in the town of Bone, along the main Phillipeville road. Sadly David Dawnay had left the regiment, having been promoted to second-in-command of the 23rd Armoured Brigade and Lord Shayne O'Neil had taken his place as Colonel of the North Irish Horse, while I was now Captain and Adjutant. The grovelling had finally paid off!

Awaiting shipment to Italy for a further bout of active service, we enjoyed a good time just playing the fool. Wonderful swimming on the glorious beaches where an attractive French lass served us with piping hot jam omelettes[2] together with a glass of chilled Rosé. Absolutely delicious compared with bully beef and mugs of tepid cook-house tea laced with bromide and dished up by a boss-eyed batman. Coming to think of it, 'Sa mère' wasn't half a bad sort either, but she was too busy slaving over a hot kitchen stove folding strawberry jam into the piping hot omelettes.

An hilarious holiday in Algiers followed when Dick Hern, John Behr and I were overpowered by three formidable ladies in a sordid brothel. Frankly my intended terrified me more than any of the Krauts on Longstop Hill. However, we were able to make a strategic withdrawal from the knocking shop just in time to retain our honour as officers and gentlemen!

---

[2] see Appendix 3, page 92, for the recipe.

Chapter Six

BATTLE OF THE HITLER LINE

In May 1944 orders were issued for our regiment to prepare for embarkation to Italy. Half the troops would sail from Bone and half from Algiers, converging at Lucera near Foggia, where we were to carry out exercises with the 2nd Canadian Infantry Brigade. Finally, we were to muster en bloc four miles out of Pontecarvo to prepare for the Battle of the Hitler Line.

This encounter was to differ in every aspect from the final phase of Longstop Hill, which was fought over a very narrow front, the onslaught about to be waged would be along a three thousand yard front involving two regiments of tanks supporting a full battalion of infantry apiece, both strengthened by a barrage of some 600 artillery pieces.

Once again I shall attempt to recall only the sector of the battle in which I was personally involved. To tell the full story of the action along the entire front would be guesswork on my part, or learned at a later date from the official battle reports. Such reports, in my humble opinion, were invariably exaggerated and grossly inaccurate, turning military failures into glorious victories. The brasshats usually emerged with unwarranted credit and undue honour for brilliant planning and direction of the forces under their command. At the end of the day, I suppose those who perished at least departed in a blaze of glory, thus easing the distress for their relatives and loved ones.

At that time I was second-in-command of 'B' squadron which had been appointed to support the Canadian Seaforth Highlanders on the left of the line. Intelligence reports were contradictory and confusing, indicating that the stronghold was not fully manned.

49

The signs were that withdrawals from the front were taking place, while another source of information reported heavy sightings of enemy tanks and other weapons in the area.

Reconnaissance reports helped to complicate the picture even further with rumours of strong permanent defences bristling with all manner of anti-tank and machine gun emplacements with permanent underground living accommodation for their crews. These were reputed to have taken months to construct in concrete and steel and cleverly camouflaged to obliterate all evidence of their presence. Finally, there was supposed to be a heavily mined anti-tank ditch, also well concealed, covering the full width of the area.

However, we would soon learn the full strength of the enemy defences. At mid-day the following morning an 'O' group had been called up to receive orders for the imminent attack. It transpired that at first light on May 23rd our regiment would link up with their infantry on a prearranged start line, then stand by to await the signal to attack. The start line was approximately two hundred yards short of a densely thick belt of woodland, estimated to be four hundred yards from the final objective. This open area had been described in some quarters as "a burial ground for the tanks".

That afternoon, when all the troop leaders and myself were gathered around Major Gordon Russell, our Squadron Leader, to receive our orders for the following morning, a dispatch rider roared up with a signal from Brigade Headquarters to Major Russell, concerning a certain Captain Pope. It read, 'Report Intelligence HQ 1800 hours equipped to carry out reconnaissance patrol with composite force'.

I thought to myself, 'Holy Mackerel that means me, it must be some dreadful mistake.' However, Gordon, having read the instruction said, 'There's no mistake.

Don't be such a wimp. You'll be all right. Besides, your efforts could well benefit us all."

Off I went looking a right pillock with an oversized steel helmet down over my ears, a gas mask strapped to my chest and a revolver slung round my waist. My half-witted batman assured me this was the correct gear for a recce patrol.

On arrival at HQ, as luck would have it, I spotted David Dawnay, who by this time was a Brigadier and second-in-command of the 23rd Armoured Brigade. Hurriedly, I explained that I had a gut feeling we were about to set forth on a suicide mission. David explained sympathetically that the order for the recce in each sector had come from the Divisional Commander and therefore he was powerless to revoke this instruction. However, he added with a wink, "I'll put you in charge of the outfit Mike, then you can conduct the exercise as you see fit!"

There were eight of us in all, two engineers, armed with mine detectors, two foot sloggers, two gunners, a fellow called Geoff Franklin, a personal friend from another tank regiment, and myself. Our instructions were to proceed through the wood until we reached the open ground, then weigh up the enemy defences before returning to base. I thought to myself, 'Not bloody likely. I shall be crying wolf long before then!"

Arriving at the edge of the wood we spotted a narrow ride running through the dense trees and I told the two engineers to press on ahead with the mine detectors, while the rest of us would follow behind at a sensible distance. I kidded myself that being in charge of the outfit I would have best control from a tailed off position! As it was a very humid and steamy evening I was soon dripping with sweat, so I discarded my gas mask into the undergrowth. Come to think of it, my perspiring was almost certainly caused by fear and not the humid conditions.

We had gone only twenty yards when I thought I heard German voices. They appeared to come from up in the trees, forwards and directly above us. Clearly, I was not mistaken because the entire party froze almost simultaneously, then slowly turned around to await my instructions. Without hesitation I made a hand signal above my head to withdraw rapidly. When well clear of the wood I called Brigade HQ on the radio to report that I had cancelled the patrol and we were returning to base. Altogether a nerve-racking experience. Nevertheless, it did seem to cure those among us suffering from constipation.

When we got back, a young lieutenant from the Intelligence Corps, barely dry behind his ears, called me to his office for interrogation. When I told him that we had heard German voices up in the trees he grinned disbelievingly and said: "Captain, are you quite certain they were not pigeons billing and cooing to each other?" Insulted by such an insinuation, I thought to myself, 'You conniving little creep', did a quick about turn without uttering a word and stormed out of his office, slamming the door as hard as I could behind me. I later very much regretted not letting him have the cream of my vocabulary.

The next morning the tanks were all lined up ready to roll by 05.30 hours. As dawn was breaking we received the order to pull out of harbour. It was a depressing and miserable morning with slight drizzle and a heavy mist, making visibility very poor indeed. As we trundled down a long dusty track towards the prearranged start line we spotted the Seaforth Highlanders with whom we were to link up. They waved cheerfully, almost as if they were looking forward to a scrap and were anxious to get cracking.

Just then, as I turned around to check if all our tanks were following safely, I spotted what I thought was an American truck overtaking the column at a rate of knots. As it was heading straight in the direction of the enemy lines I guessed the driver was either lost, mad, or drunk or all three and waved him down furiously. Coming to a grinding halt a large black Yank in a baseball cap leaned out of the cab as I yelled, "And where the bloody hell do you think you're going, fella?" Agitatedly he replied: "I don't know where I'm Goddam going, buddy, but with all the crap flying around I only know I'm getting the hell out of here."

Without further ado he revved up furiously and taking off in a cloud of dust, swung left-handedly along the cart track parallel to the wood we were about to penetrate, before disappearing over the brow and out of sight. I often wonder where that fella had come from, where he was supposed to be going and with what purpose in mind. I had a feeling he just didn't care any more and was making one last frantic dash for freedom. I sincerely hope he made it!

The clouds of dust our tanks began to create quickly drew enemy fire. Then our own artillery opened up and for the next half hour the barrage exchange was horrendous. At times, I wondered if the enemy were deadly accurate, or if our own shells were falling short. In fact, I voiced my doubts over the radio in the hope our 'Sunray' might ask the artillery to increase the range by a few hundred yards. I had a nasty feeling the shells falling around us had the Union Jack stamped on them!

A temporary lull followed. We grabbed the opportunity to sort ourselves out into some sort of battle order, facing towards the cursed wood. Now and again, for a brief moment, our tank commanders opened up their turret flaps and poked their heads out. To remain closed down for any length of time, peering through periscopes, caused them to become disorientated. At that moment a single rifle shot rang out and Graham Brown, the troop leader in the penultimate tank to mine, slumped down into his turret.

Our fears were confirmed when the grief stricken voice of Graham's gunner came over the air. "My boss has been killed outright by a bullet through the head." Still feeling totally gutted with shock, the order to advance came over the air and, convinced that the fatal shot had almost certainly come from one of the snipers strapped to the branches in the top of the trees, I had a deadly urge to flush them out and murder the bastards.

Approaching the wood Gordon Russell, in the tank immediately on my right, called up, "Good luck Mike, I have a horrible feeling we are in for a bloodbath. Stay close and we'll support each other." As I headed straight for the narrow ride we had entered on patrol the previous evening, I said to my gunners, "Cock your machine-gun up into the air and keep spraying the top of the trees until I tell you to stop."

Visibility was now practically nil with a mixture of dust, mist and sulphur fumes lingering within the dense foliage. Although lost, somehow we managed to press on, felling trees like a herd of rampant elephants as we crashed on through the wood. We assumed that sooner or later we must inevitably hit open ground.

We counted our tanks, as one after another they groped their way out of the undergrowth, rather like rabbits being flushed from the last strip of corn at harvest. By now the barrage had subsided and apart from the roar of our engines there was an eerie and uncanny silence. I glanced across at Gordon and acknowledged a rather dubious 'so far so good' thumbs sign as he repeated the order to advance once again. We even leaned out of our turrets to cheer on the Seaforths who were now striding forward with great determination. I suspect that every man jack was praying to himself that the Germans had done a runner — when suddenly like a horrific storm of thunder

54

and lighting, all hell let loose with the entire front seeming to explode as one.

Within minutes five of our tanks had been knocked out, including Gordon's away on the right, followed almost immediately by my own. The impact of whatever struck us must have caused me to black out for a moment, as the first sound I remember was our driver shouting over the intercom. "Both our tracks have been blown off and the gun turret is jammed."

The scene all around us was of total carnage and what with the moaning and groaning from the wounded, I am sure we all thought our time had come. I was about to join my crew in a nearby shell crater when I heard oscillating from the headset of the radio which was hanging down from the turret. I grabbed it and ignoring any of the normal wireless procedure, shouted as loudly as I possibly could: "Stop anybody else coming forward, we are being annihilated from all sides." I didn't wait for an acknowledgement as I knew Dick King, our very able wireless controller, would pass on my message to all concerned. Once in the crater the noise above ground was so terrific it felt as if my eardrums were about to burst. We could hear an enormous explosion as our tanks were systematically picked off, followed by a blinding flash as they finally went up in flames. We started to discuss what to do next. Should we try to make a run for it or remain doggo until the pressure had died down? Hard to believe at the height of such a battle but either the effects of extreme exhaustion, sulphur fumes, or both, lulled all five of us into a coma-like state. When we came round some time later, there was a weird and eerie silence mixed with the stench of gun-powder. Clawing our way out of the hole a sickening scene of devastation greeted us. Our own tank was burnt out, but in a slouched position up against the leeward side of the hulk was a sergeant of the Seaforth Highlanders.

Without any obvious signs of injury he appeared to be having a quiet kip, his steel helmet tipped forward as if sheltering his eyes and his rifle lying across his lap.

I went across to him and as I lifted his helmet, instantly I knew he was not dozing but dead, very dead. Totally dejected and drained of all feelings, we started to shuffle aimlessly in the direction whence we had come, hardly caring whether we survived or perished.

Suddenly we heard the sound of a vehicle approaching at some speed. It was a blood wagon flying the Red Cross flag from the top of its wireless mast. As the driver pulled up we could see he had a full load of bodies on board, some strapped to stretchers and swathed in bandages. He cheerfully directed us to the nearest medical post a few hundred yards further back.

A team of ambulances to-ing and fro-ing indicated that we did not have far to go and we were relieved to catch sight of Padre Hughes, a lovely man equally respected by all ranks and religions. It was so very sad to see him with tears in his eyes as he reeled off, in his warm Welsh brogue, the names of his flock for whom he had performed the last rites.

Apart from our pride, my crew and I had only minor injuries, and I fancy the gash on my leg was inflicted by a glancing blow from a protruding track pin as I took a dive from the top of the tank. The medical officer peered at our wounds and merely recommended that we be evacuated after they had been dressed. I enquired from the Padre if he had any news of Gordon Russell and was greatly relieved to learn he was still alive, albeit in a critical condition.

Quite soon I became separated from my crew and ended up in an Officers' Rest Home down in Naples. After a few nights of solid kip, a gutful of pasta and a surfeit of local vino at the Albergo Ponchini, I just knew I had to get the hell out of this depressing environment where the majority of inmates, plus the dithering doctors with the shakes, appeared destined to follow the slogan 'See Naples and die' rather than be forced to suffer the terrors of war ever again.

Not me, thank God. I was feeling fine albeit no longer willing to volunteer for a scrap. However, the quack told me I had to remain off duty for at least a fortnight before he could discharge me. There and then I decided to do a runner early the next morning before anyone surfaced. Transport was a big problem. But as luck would have it, I was having a final jar down in the town that evening, when I heard an American airman say, while sitting at the bar with a demanding-looking tart wrapped around him, "Not tonight honey, at first light I'm off to the sharp end to murder a few more Boche." I wormed my way into the conversation and soon had the promise of a lift. The red-headed pilot proceeded to get legless before being dragged out of the bar and up the stairs exclaiming, "Quanta costa?" I thought to myself, 'bang goes my lift.'

However, to my amazement, as I headed down the street at a good half speed after baling out from the nuthouse at first light, the Yank appeared around the corner, honking the horn of his Jeep furiously and shouting, "Climb aboard buddy, and hold tight." The journey back to his airbase near Aquino was hectic to say the least. Nevertheless, it was a great feeling to be rejoining those taking an active part. My new mucker was as wild as a hawk but an amusing character and we agreed to meet up again very shortly.

I found my squadron, or what was left of it, harboured nearby, having been pulled out of the line to rest and reform. Many more good friends than I expected were conspicuous by their absence, as the final score of the dead and wounded had been much greater than first feared. In fact, I learned that on the evening following the Battle of the Hitler Line thirty four officers and men of the North Irish Horse had been laid to rest in a private sector of the cemetery reserved for the 2nd Brigade of the Canadian Infantry. This burial ground lies four and a half miles south of Pontecarvo and is said to be enclosed on three sides by beautiful oak trees, the open side looking across the Lire Valley towards the historic Monastery Hill at Monte Cairo. To seal their gratitude and respect the Canadians honoured their comrades by granting the North Irish Horse the right to display the famous Maple Leaf insignia.

The atmosphere within the squadron compound was naturally gloomy and subdued, so after a couple of days I decided to pop over the visit my cheerful Yankee chum with a few bottles of hooch to thank him for his kindness. On arrival at his base I enquired from the orderly on the gate, could he direct me to the quarters of Flight Lieutenant 'Red' Herrin. From the look on the fellow's face his reply was inevitable. "Sorry buddy boy, Red bought it last night when out on a solo sortie. He blasted two of the bastards out of the sky only to be shot up the arse when returning to base."

A few weeks later, when the regiment was up to full strength and ready to go back into action, our Colonel, Shayne O'Neill, returned from hospital, having had all his teeth replaced, to resume command. He invited me to become his adjutant, but not for long. One morning he announced he was popping out to reconnoitre a river crossing. I asked if he wished me to accompany him but he replied, "Oh don't bother Mike. I'll only be gone for a short while and besides the scout car is too cramped for three." A single stray shell landed slap on his vehicle killing both Shayne and his driver outright. When I heard the tragic news I just knew my lucky horse-shoe had been at work once again!

I then took over as adjutant to his successor, Colonel Tony Llewellyn-Palmer, a brave and brilliant soldier who was to become a great personal friend with whom

I served until long after hostilities had finally ceased. In such a comparatively safe and sheltered task I was seldom required to take part in the thick of the action up front. So neither my nerve, nor the power of the horse-shoe implant, were to be put to the test again. Maybe just as well, as I was starting to have doubts about the former. I felt I might need a fair few slugs of powerful tincture before charging into battle shouting the odds!

The same feeling, I imagine, felt by a jump jockey who had survived a number of scary falls and was now down at the start sitting on a sketchy jumper about to compete in a novice chase. Not exactly cowardly fear, but a feeling of reluctance, apprehension and an urge to take a pull, rather than kick on with gay abandon!

Chapter Seven

THE WAR IS OVER

Finally, in May 1945, the eagerly awaited order, 'Stand Down' indicated that the War was over. After the regiment had been demobilised we came to rest in the vast Grand Hotel, practically on the beach at the seaside resort of Rimini. We were given various mundane and boring tasks not worthy of mention, with the exception of one which proved to be most fortuitous, particularly for the horsy types who couldn't wait to climb back into the saddle.

As Adjutant I had received an order from Brigade to provide two officers, a sergeant and a dozen other ranks to proceed to Padua, just North of the river Po, to shepherd a large consignment of German prisoners down to a new encampment near Cesena. The consignment consisted of some 500 prisoners, together with 1,500 horses, ponies and mules, plus their wagons and equipment—all part of a German Pack Transport battalion equipped to supply fighting forces in mountainous country with fuel and ammunition.

It was estimated that the task would take about fourteen days. Our Colonel, Tony Llewellyn-Palmer, suggested I should ask Dick Hern and my brother Barry to handle the task, as they would be just the lads to select and acquire some horses for an equine venture we had in mind. In fact, four stables had been urgently erected in an old boat house bordering the beaches in readiness to receive a quartet of horses from the Colonel's previous regiment, the 16/5th King's Dragoon Guards.

There was considerable secrecy surrounding these horses, especially the mare, Farina. The other three were Nera, Rhami and Tedeschi. All four had been removed from the Royal stables of the King of Italy, Victor Emmanuel III. Farina, a grey mare with the Royal crest branded on her jowl, was said to be the King's personal charger.

Because she was apparently a super ride with perfect manners II Duce Benito Mussolini, the greedy self-elected dictator, virtually took the mare over as his own. That was before he was sacked and subsequently strung up.

Four welcome arrivals from the Royal Stables of the King of Italy: left to right, Tedeschi and John Behr, Nera and myself, Farina ridden by Tony Llewellyn Palmer and Rhami with Dick Hern on board.

The Italians were now our allies and rumour had it Sir Winston Churchill had issued a direct order to our Army Commander for the mare named Farina, which had gone missing from the stables of King Victor Emmanuel to be returned to her rightful owner forthwith.

Not wishing to part with the mare, and having little respect for the Italians at that time, various excuses were given for the inability to carry out the instruction, hence the panic for a rapid change of stables. One can only imagine that our Prime Minister felt duty bound to humour King Victor Emmanuel III in view of his country's sudden change of heart, causing the elaborate command performance involving the mare.

So off went Dick and Barry to Padua. On arrival they reported back that among the rabble of mules and mountain ponies there were quite a number of respectable horses, especially those belonging to the senior officers of the outfit. It was agreed by Dick and Barry that they would take it in turns to try out a different horse each day, when riding on well ahead of the column to reconnoitre a suitable camp to harbour for the night. By doing so a fair few likely steeds could be earmarked for our purposes.

By the time the column eventually reached its destination a string of some eighteen horses of various shapes and sizes had been selected. At least half a dozen of these were thoroughbreds, or very nearly, and suitable for racing. The others would certainly made either good show-jumpers or riding school hacks. I should add that Dick and Barry had sportingly selected and named a mare for me personally. She was a big flashy chestnut called Red Sails and had four white socks. She seemed an ever goer and was most likely the pick of the bunch.

One evening, when it was nearly dark, Barry happened to spot a couple of prisoners humping two metal boxes out of the back of the vehicles in the column into a deep ditch at the side of the road. At first Barry paid little regard but on reflection he thought, "I wonder what these conniving Krauts are up to? I bet there's something valuable in those crates. Maybe they are being dumped only to be picked up later by an accomplice."

62

Comrades in Arms: the author with Tony Finch-Noyes and Dick Hern.

On checking the vehicle in question it turned out to be an imprest van in which the pay for the entire German battalion had been carried. Barry lost no time returning to the spot where the boxes had been dumped and very soon had the two heavy containers under cover of tarpaulin in the rear of his Jeep. Each was fitted with strong double padlocks and could not be forced open to check the contents. However, Barry was confident they would be stuffed with cash, bundles and bundles of lovely lire.

Away down in Rimini I was more than surprised when a delivery of two metal boxes appeared addressed to 'Captain Michael Pope, Adjutant to North Irish

Horse' and the name of the consignee given merely as B.L.B.P. Those being Barry's initials I sent for his batman and instructed him to store the boxes under his master's bed and keep a close eye on them until his return. I assumed they contained various items of loot he and Dick had filched on their travels down from Padua and gave the matter no further thought. Some time later when Barry eventually returned, I inquired what treasures he had stored but was fairly certain it was lovely lolly. He went on to explain how he had come by the chests and added that he would have to get a large hacksaw from the fitters' store before he could remove the padlocks. A strange look came over his face when he added, "You don't think those boxes could be booby-trapped do you?" We had a good laugh and I suggested he should send his batman, rather a simple fellow, down to the beach early one morning when nobody was about and instruct him to open them up!

Nevertheless, the thought of some booby-trap device must have seriously entered Barry's mind, because he admitted sometime later that he had, in fact, pulled the boxes gently from under his bed, then carefully sawn through the clasps, before attaching a long length of wire to the staple of each lock. He then retired a safe distance along the passage before giving a sharp tug. Not a sound! When he returned to his room what a wonderful sight, thousands of crisp new notes stacked in piles. Likewise the second box, stuffed with notes of even larger denominations. What a sight for sore eyes!

Highly ambitious plans were now well advanced, not only for the stable block to be extended in the boathouse on the beach, but also for the resurrection of the old trotting track at Ravenna which had suffered considerable damage during the hostilities. Other schemes included the conversion of three trucks into horseboxes and the financial brains of the regiment were working on plans to operate a Totalisator.

When all the projects had finally been completed, the North Irish Horse would have its own training facilities on the beaches at Rimini and the use of the racecourse at Ravenna on which to run its race meetings. Dick and Barry had decided to set up camp on the track to supervise at first hand the necessary repairs to be carried out. Labour would present no problems as many of the prisoners were more than pleased to come over each day in their own transport to lend a hand under the supervision of a few 'trusties'.

The track itself had taken a frightful hammering, firstly by shelling and subsequently when used by the Germans as a car park for their heavy vehicles. Under the relentless pounding in wet weather the surface had become like concrete. Luckily, the actual stands and supporting buildings had not suffered too badly and could soon be restored to their former glory.

Dick and Barry had now moved in to start operations. They slept on top of the stands in their camp beds and had most of their meals, consisting of pasta and macaroni, at a small eating and drinking café called the Albergo Cappello down in the town. There the also consumed vast quantities of local vino, and when something stronger was required a bottle of Egg Nog would be produced from under the counter. The intrepid racecourse constructors found there was no shortage of feminine company willing to befriend two such handsome English Officers, making life not totally devoid of pleasure.

Somehow, a certain Major Morgan had managed to get in on the act. He was permanently saturated and at first light he could be sighted on top of the stands emerging from beneath his mosquito net, desperate for a drag on a cigarette, followed by a swig from his vino bottle. A keen hunting man he would stagger home in the early hours and encourage Barry's Alsatian dog Loot to flush out stray cats, blowing his hunting horn and hollering at the top of his voice until the poor moggies escaped hissing and spitting up into the tops of the trees.

Barry Pope with the appropriately named Alsatian dog 'Loot' whose previous owner, a German, was by this time in a prison camp.

To rectify the very firm going on the racetrack a contraption of heavy steel harrows was constructed out of a load of pickaxe heads, ingeniously welded together and towed round and round by a half track vehicle. Dust in hot weather also presented a problem. That was soon overcome by attaching a set of wide sprinklers to the rear of a large water cart which would cover a circuit of the course between races.

A fence expertly constructed by Dick Hern.

Probably the most professional task undertaken involved the four steeplechase fences, built from scratch out of bundles of juniper shrub under the expert supervision of Dick Hern. They really were a work of art, with an inviting slope tempting man and beast to stand off and have a cut. Lengths of running rails were to be erected and painted. The original number board was in a very sorry state but apart from general repairs the only major problem over on the stands side of the course was the ladies' lavatory. It had taken a terrible bashing. Once again, cunning improvisation prevailed. A number of well worn seats were pilfered from a local builder's yard and let into a wide plant of wood cleverly erected to conceal an open earth closer beneath. With an artistic slap of paint the powder room was ready for action!

While all this work was in progress Dick and Barry had become friends with Signor Zotti, a powerful character who had a lot of influence in the town. In peacetime he was a big noise in the trotting world and was anxious to transfer the best of the horses he had left up to Milano where trotting racing was still operating.

It was suggested that we should loan him our new converted horse-boxes to transport his animals in return for arranging an exchange of Barry's 'hot' seemingly bottomless pit. Both the trip to Milano and the bank transaction passed without a hitch with no questions asked.

While all involved at Ravenna were now working feverishly to complete the racecourse in time for the opening meeting, the activity down at Rimini was equally hectic in preparation for the big day. The horses had done well, except that the insides of some were like 'grass through a goose' due to their diet. Rather moderate barley and a type of chopped soft meadow hay known as tiffin were the only rations supplied by the Army and we urgently required some decent bruised oats and a good hard hay, especially for the thoroughbreds.

Our improvised stable block in the boathouse on the beach at Rimini.

Word had it that some of the Italian farmers out in the country might be persuaded to exchange barley for the forage we required and the Colonel suggested that Dick and Barry, now back at headquarters, should take a couple of days off to seek out a few likely barterers. Off they went in a three-ton truck with orders not to return without a full load of decent hay and oats, no matter whether acquired by fair means or foul.

After a couple of sorties the procurers appeared to have the matter well in hand. Apparently, the modus operandi was that they would approach a likely farm, where Dick would let roar, "Dove Patronia, scambiare orzo per avena?" If given the customary response, "Nienti, nienti, le tedesci portrari vi, bovini, gallini, tutti tutti," the hiding place of the forage with the help of a good 'nose' would be revealed without further delay. Having loaded up the truck, handed over a worthless document signed 'Happy Christmas,' 'How's Yer Father,' 'Charlie the Chinese Cook' or some equally nonsensical signature, Dick and Barry would head off like bats out of hell. As Adjutant at Regimental HQ, I was beginning to come in for a fair amount of flak. Finally, I received a visit from the military police querying if I was aware that two of our officers had procured forage from Italian farmers using meaningless documentation. Of course I denied any knowledge of any such disgraceful behaviour, unbecoming of officers and gentlemen, and promised to look into the matter. 'Don't worry, I will guarantee to take the appropriate action,' I vowed, which I did by slipping the documents in question through the shredder in the orderly room before my staff had sight of them.

I next received an order from Brigade to the effect that all current notes of Lira money held by officers and other ranks be handed in within twenty-four hours, after which a search had to be held to ensure the order had been carried out. Panic stations ensured as I signed the declaration stated that no such monies had been handed in or found, knowing full well a sizeable tin crammed with notes[3] remained secreted beneath Barry's and my pit.

At the poker school that evening I mentioned the episode to a very senior officer and good friend of mine, just in case I might need to be bailed out. Jokingly, he said: "You deserve to be court martialled, but if you have any spare Lira I could do with a sub as my son's fees at Eton are enormous and long overdue!"

Mind you, I had been grovelling under my bed and dipping into the old tin chest myself for quite some time so the old nest egg was somewhat depleted. Our Colonel was a very keen, albeit erratic poker player, and I was delighted when he started inviting me to go along and take a hand in his high powered school. The players, more often than not, would consist of a brace of Brigadiers, the odd General, Tony Llewellyn-Palmer and myself. Tony was a fearless gambler, especially after four or five tumblers of scotch, but seldom made a profit, normally an alarming loss.

Colonel Tony Llewellyn-Palmer (nearest) with his fellow race stewards and poker-playing chums.

---

[3] ...one of which appears on the cover of this book!

When the game folded he would look across the table at me over his empty glass and say: "Mike, old boy, I seem a bit short of cash, will you please settle on my behalf?" After a couple of such fruitless forays I began to feel the main purpose for my presence could possibly be as a money lender, although 'lender' was hardly appropriate as seldom were the loans reimbursed.

To be fair, Tony was fully aware that the cash was decidedly 'dodgy' and that there was plenty more where that came from. Nevertheless, my envious muckers never missed an opportunity to jibe that being the Colonel's 'banker' helped me to retain my cushy job as Adjutant. Come to think of it, there might have been a modicum of truth in that theory. Never mind, Tony was a grand fellow and I must enjoyed those snobby evenings among the brasshats at brother Barry's expense!

It wasn't long before the Red Cap returned. He said, with a bit of a smirk on his face: "I have received a complaint from a young signorina who states that when riding her bicycle along the main road between Rimini and Ravenna two English Officers approached from behind in an open Jeep. The one in the passenger seat shouted to the driver: 'Slow down and pull over as we pass that lass on the bog wheel'. With that the passenger gave the girl a smack on the buttocks. I mentioned this accusation to Dick and Barry as I thought it would amuse them. Roars of laughter were followed by the response, "Yes, and a damn pretty young lass she was too."

All was now set for the grand opening at the racecourse in Ravenna. Dick had booked himself to ride Birdcatcher and Victoria, Barry had settled for Pitter-Pat, Tony Finch-Noyes was on Stubbles and I was fortunate enough to be having a bump round on Red Sails and Farina. The racecard included races over fences and on the flat, varying in distance from five furlongs to two miles. Four high ranking officers acted as stewards and controlled the operation well, in spite of some rather rough riding, skulduggery and extremely expressive and colourful language.

Michael Pope (left on Farina) and Dick Hern on Birdcatcher jumping the last fence at Ravenna.

A very good crowd of spectators turned up and bet freely on the Tote, which was manipulated skilfully by the members of the regiment. A handsome profit was duly promised to the regiment's Benevolent Fund. However, the adjudicator reported that a member of staff had been suspected of slipping cash to his pals on the outside. Lo and behold at the next meeting the handsome profit was reduced to an equally depressing loss, and the Benevolent Fund missed out. Unfortunately, the matter reaches the ear of the Brigade Commander: who roared "Disgraceful behaviour! Heads must roll!" Being very loyal to his old regiment and a passionate racing man, he agreed to forget the episode if we scrapped the Tote forthwith.

Basil Cooper leading Victoria, ridden by Dick Hern chatting to Colonel Tony Llewellyn-Palmer.

Nevertheless, it had been a great day for all concerned. Dick, balanced on his home-made racing saddle, which he described as the 'beetle' and waving his pliant cosh known as the 'bullsprick', rode a winning double in great style.

Brother Barry won with ease on Pitter-Pat while I, riding like a demented cowboy, managed to scrub a couple more past the post for the North Irish Horse. As a matter of interest the 'beetle' was no more than pieces of felt cleverly sewn onto a saddle tree with two large rings serving as stirrups. It was very light and made to Dick's own design by one of the welders in the workshop. Not a Whippy or an Owen, but perfectly serviceable for the job in hand.

Horses in transit courtesy of the North Irish Horse initiative.

The 'bullsprick' was made for a mature bull's penis, officially known as a 'Pizzle' when used for flogging humans. It was sliced down into strips, salted, then hung up to dry with a heavy weight on the end to stretch and strengthen it. The strips were plaited to produce a very flexible whip with a knob on the end. When waved furiously it made a very effective swishing sound, inflicting only the minimal amount of pain and causing virtually no marking. Perhaps this is the design the Stewards of the Jockey Club have long been seeking!

That night we all got legless and congratulated Dick and Barry for their graft, improvisation and cunning, which had made the whole project possible and such as success. I have forgotten to mention that while all this activity was going on a number of officers, including Johnnie Behr, who had never had a leg over a horse before, had been taught to ride down on the beach by our resident expert instructor—The Galloping Major himself—Dick Hern.

Tony Finch-Noyes snatches a stylish victory on Stubbles.

Although we had experienced our fair share of fighting, fun and frolic, we were elated at the thought of returning to Blighty to be re-united with our families once more. God bless those poor devils who were not so lucky.

Farina with Michael Pope on board gets well away to make all, in spite of the pilot. (Note the Italian Royal brand on the mare's jowl.)

A column of some 500 prisoners with an assortment of 1500 horses, ponies, mules and wagons was escorted down from Padua, crossing the River Po via the Bailey Bridge and on to the POW camp at Cesena near Rimini. This arduous task, which turned out to be a stroke of luck for the racing fraternity, was entrusted to Dick Hern and Barry Pope.

Chapter Eight

ENTENTE CORDIAL

Dick Hern saves the day for the North Irish Horse by snatching third place on Birdcatcher.

Our regiment had now moved up from Rimini to Austria and with many of us due to return home it was good news to receive an invitation from General Sir Richard McCreery to take part in a race meeting he was sponsoring for the Allied Forces on the racecourse at Vienna. It would be a fitting farewell to arms and our Colonel Tony Llewellyn-Palmer gave us carte blanche to assemble a team. We rounded up the usual cowboys, Dick Hern, Basil Cooper, my brother Barry and I, plus, of course, the Colonel himself.

Off we went with an assortment of vehicles, including three horse-boxes carrying six horses, their forage and tack, with bedrolls and rations for ourselves, plus staff car and a couple of Jeeps. It was a long, arduous journey. We encountered considerable difficulty at the check point entry to the Russian zone. However, we eventually arrived unscathed at Vienna racecourse where the horses and their lads were to be accommodated. We deposited our travelling circus then set off in search of our digs. It turned out to be a vast cavernous hotel in the centre of the City, totally devoid of furniture and without any services whatsoever.

As ever the attentive adjutant, I made it my duty to see that the Colonel was provided with his creature comforts, being without his batman. Not that he was in the least particular. Somewhere to lay his head, a washbowl, plenty of grub (preferably cold chicken), a liberal supply of whisky, cigarettes galore and he was perfectly content. He was inclined to mumble through his moustache and when 'having a scrape' as he called it, with cigarette still hanging from his mouth, his instructions were practically indecipherable, I understood him to say, "Mike, make sure I have a large comfy mistress, and don't forget I like a bit of breast."

I was always aware that he had a keen eye for the fairer sex but never before did I hear him allude to sex in such a direct and forthright manner. I though to myself, where the hell do I find a suitable woman prepared to provide her services on a hard floor, and I wonder what nationality, age or colour he has in mind. It always infuriated him to have to repeat his orders but on this occasion I plucked up the courage to recap with him. He roared: "Are you going deaf or something Mike? Surely it is not too much to ask for a mattress to lie on, and a cold chicken to keep the wolf from the door without making such a bloody palaver about it." The Colonel thought it was the most hilarious misunderstanding and seldom missed an opportunity to take the piss out of me in the Officers' Mess when the port was circulating.

Having tired of slaving over an oil stove, we decided to see if we could find a café, and as we strode along the street, smartly kitted out in our officers uniforms, we were confronted by three very scruffy Russian soldiers, clearly full of drink and armed with fearsome-looking weapons, shuffling along towards us. We half expected them to step off the pavement and allow us to pass, but by their aggressive attitude they intended we should be the ones to give way. Hurriedly, we jumped from the curb as they sneered and jeered in a threatening fashion. The krauts we had been fighting were fearsome enough, but they were ponces compared with these horrifying individuals. Quite a number of them were Mongolians in tatty Russian uniforms, with cruel-looking faces and mean slit eyes. We decided it would be wise to smile, nod and adopt an entente cordial attitude at all times from now on. The next day we had a runner in each of the races, although I can only remember three of them by name. Dick Hern was on 'Birdcatcher', Barry rode 'Pitter-Pat' and I was to pilot 'Red Sails' in the big race, the Dick McCreery Cup. My mare was much fancied to win, but I had my reservations as she had moved very poorly during her final gallop two days before.

Vienna Racecourse *in 1945, the venue for the Allied Forces' race meeting sponsored by General Richard McCreery.*

At the entrance to the racecourse stands, which were festooned with flags of all the Allied nations, stood an enormous Russian General, surrounded by guards armed to the teeth. Hardly a spectacle one expected to meet face to face on a friendly racecourse. We saluted smartly, smiled sheepishly and moved on rapidly to pay our respects to our host General McCreery. Before we eventually tracked him down we passed through various groups of more civilised military gentlemen of all ranks, jabbering away in their native tongues— French, Italian, American and a few of debatable origin, providing a truly international flavour. I suppose we were unwittingly the fore-runners of international racing. Trailblazers, if you like.

Our first two runners failed dismally, either unlucky or not good enough. I was the next big hope of the side to defend the honour of the regiment. However, on cantering down to the start my fears proved well founded. I could only pray the mare would stride out once we were underway. Never taking hold of her bridle or jumping fluently I was unable to hold my place and got totally baulked going into the open ditch. I shouted in no uncertain terms at the two guilty riders, thinking they must be ignorant foreigners. When pushing on upsides to give them another earful, I immediately recognised one as Brigadier Peter Payne-Galway and the other his mucker, Brigadier Roscoe Harvey.

Approaching the penultimate obstacle I decided to drop out. Joe Hartingan, a good friend from the 12th Lancers, went by with a double fistful riding 'Jumbo', owned by our host. I yelled to him, "I've had it, kick on Joe, you'll trot up if you don't fall off at the last." On pulling up, 'Red Sails' was lame and as I hopped down to lead her in the two Brigadiers rode up. I thought to myself, now I'm for it. I'm sure to get a good bollocking for giving them both barrels. On the contrary, they both apologised for squeezing me out, adding that they were knackered and hoped they were not responsible for laming my mare. Two truly gallant Officers and Gentlemen!

Alas in the next race brother Barry suffered a disappointing ride on 'Pitter-Pat'. All our hopes hung on Dick Hern and 'Birdcatcher' in the last. Neither let the side down and snatching third place they retrieved the reputation of the North Irish Horse. That evening we were all invited to a celebration party at the Schonbrunn Palace. Apparently the Russian General Kurasov had agreed to attend, provided a red carpet was rolled out for his arrival. On hearing that General McCreery was to present a large cup to the winner the Ruski ordered his ADC to obtain an even bigger one. Sweating profusely the aide returned, clutching a vast silver cup inscribed 'The Imperial Hotel', obviously filched from the vaults of the hotel on the Ringstrasse, which was the Headquarters of the Russian Army in Austria.

The event was going swimmingly, a most enjoyable and cordial evening until the Russian General, now sodden with drink, began to boast about the plundering of Berlin by his army, when more than a million women of all ages were raped by his soldiers. The party broke up before another war broke out. On descending the vast marble staircase, one of our party was still smoking his cigar when he spotted a large notice, 'Nicht rauchen'. In panic and with no suitable receptacle in sight he stubbed out the butt of his cigar between the buttocks of the large cherub adorning the pillar at the bottom of the stairs. A chum following close behind whipped out a serviette from his pocket, which he had pinched from the dinner table as a souvenir of the proceedings, to wipe the cherub's bum, remarking as he did so how realistic these Viennese statues were.

Me and Red Sails before the start of the ill-fated race.

The bizarre Russian General apart, it was an unforgettable adventure and as we were about to leave the Palace, a young Hungarian lad working in the stable asked if we would take him back home with us to work in our stables. He was so insistent we agreed. However he declined to tell us he would have difficulty getting through the Russian check points.

We stuck him under the straw in one of the trucks and told him to bide quiet. All went well and he proved to be a good keen working lad. Sadly, it did not last long and he went missing one night without trace. We often wonder what fate befell him!

Chapter Nine

BACK TO BLIGHTY :
HOME SWEET HOME

The incentive to survive had proved worthwhile. I was back home at long last with family, horses, ponies, dogs, cats and one remaining budgie—not forgetting the faithful little old car, an Austin 7 (ALD 795). She had served the entire family, young and old, proudly and well, all through the war. With the desperate shortage of petrol the game little engine had struggled manfully against the 'four-in-one' hill to the nearest village of Streatley, on a mixture of paraffin diluted with a chaser of petrol.

Home Sweet Home was a lovely, friendly, warm dry old farmhouse. Oozing charm and character with an assortment of barns and buildings down in a valley, surrounded by some twenty acres of paddocks and woodland.

While I had been absent the family had made a brave attempt to convert a derelict barn into a dwelling house and some cattle stalls into a stable yard to house a dozen or so racehorses. This was no mean feat as all the necessary materials had either fallen off the back of a lorry or had been acquired from the black market.

With or without planning permission we pledged to complete the job within a couple of months. Meanwhile, I applied to Messrs Weatherby, secretariat to the Jockey Club, for a trainer's licence in readiness for the big day. The application we considered a mere formality in view of the circumstances. To our horror and disgust, a fast refusal came by return of post. The reason stated—I did not have sufficient horses to train.

True, there were only five and some of those were a trifle suspect, but if I did not have a licence how the hell could I set about getting more owners and horses? It was a terrible blow to us all and I really believe my contempt for Weatherbys and the Jockey Club was even greater than my hate for the Germans I had been attempting to murder for the last few years.

I telephoned 15, Cavendish Square every day to let the thoughtless dictators know what I thought of them. My wife and mother, a formidable pair of ladies when ruffled, especially concerning an injustice to one of their tribe, were suitably incensed, firing off a very strong but respectful letter to the reigning monarch, King George VI.

I had changed tactics, meanwhile, grovelling rather than abusing the powers that be, just in case they were bent on revenge for the caning my old man had given them in the High Court when suing for libel on my behalf.

However, no further necessity for abuse or speculation was needed. Postman Fred pedalled over the hill with the required document. No explanation, no apology. Who cared. I had a licence to train racehorses and that was all that mattered.

We were all so convinced His Majesty had been responsible for instructing the autocratic Stewards of the Jockey Club to do the decent thing, that we got seriously sloshed and sang 'God Save The King' with great gusto.

Mind you, the ladies who scribed the letter had made much of the fact that I had been a member of the cavalry troop responsible for protecting the Royal Household at night when in residence at Windsor Park. Thankfully, no mention had been made of just how I would have gone about repelling a swarm of German parachutists floating down out of the sky, mounted on an ancient charger, armed only with a sword. Just as well perhaps. But the stable yard was now up and running with a few decent owners showing interest.

One was Edwin McAlpine, a major owner of horses under both rules. He became a member of the Jockey Club, which was a help, and a more loyal owner one could not wish to train for.

Out of the blue, I had a call from a fellow called Ramsay Miller, a pre-War mucker and a very able veterinary surgeon. He enquired if I would care to ride a couple of horses at the Vale of Aylesbury point-to-point at Kingston Blount, not far from Streatley.

He explained that he vetted the horses when they had changed hands and the new owners had asked him to recommend a pilot to ride them in their races. Before agreeing I asked if the animals had been well schooled. Ramsay jokingly replied, "Don't be so choosy, anyone would think you were Frenchie Nicholson and Shaun Magee rolled into one, instead of a chalk jockey whose only claim to fame has been to punch home a few old screws stolen from the Krauts."

On a serious note, Ramsay said he knew nothing of the horses' jumping capabilities, but if one could believe the previous owner, an Irish dealer, "they could jump Dublin Castle, to be sure." That should have been warning enough. Kay and I set off in ALD 795 flying along like a bird now that she was firing on regulation liquid. Both my saddles were in the back, one a comfortable lightweight hunting plate and the other a four pound buckskin.

Both had been overseas with me and were very much respected. The first of my rides was called Flyover—nothing to look at, in fact very common, ignorant and poorly turned out. Come to think of it, not unlike the owners Mr and Mrs Percy Pratt. With trepidation, I asked why the horse was equipped with an evil-looking drop nose band strapped painfully tight. The gormless woman, who never gave her arse a chance, stifled her husband's reply, "Oh, that's to keep his mouth shut." I thought, Yes, and you old man should get you one for Christmas.

On the way down to the start I very soon sussed the real reason for the horrible attachment. Galloping like the clappers, throwing his legs all over the place, I was completely out of control. When I shortened my reins in an effort to steady the brute he threw his head back into my lap and gazed skywards, pissing off again. When I gave him a bit of rein, in the hope he would drop his nut, I got the same result. I'd just about run my race by the time we got to the start. I was still getting my breath back enough to answer "Yes Sir" as the starter called out the register of runners when the next thing I knew we were off again with a vengeance.

Away he went like the wind, oblivious of whether the starter intended it to be a 'go' or not. Clearly, he's seen enough of us already and was glad to see the back of us. In the distance I heard the commentator roar from his van, "They're off and Flyover ridden by the gallant Major Pope, recently returned from active service overseas, is setting a merry gallop in the lead."

Gallant Major my arse, I thought. I've never been so scared in my life. With that 'Flyover' rooted the first fence as if it didn't exist and amidst a cloud of dust and sticks, landed in a heap on the other side of the fence punching me up around his ears. Somehow, I scrambled back into the plate, but by the time I had gathered up my reins, returned my feet to the stirrup irons and regained by equilibrium, we were careering for the next obstacle at a terrifying pace.

The horrible swine, again making no attempt to take off, crashed through the fence projecting me out of the side door. I scrambled quickly to my feet, not in an effort to remount, but to rescue my saddle before giving the horse a crack around the backside, hoping never to see the monster ever again. He was eventually caught, unharmed of course, by the Huntsman on loose horses duty, who rode back leading Flyover and carrying a mangled looking mess of a saddle, totally beyond repair.

Of course I should have refused to ride the second article, appropriately called Jumping Jack, but foolishly found myself, concussed maybe, sitting on the scales again to weigh out with the buckskin over my arm. On the way to the start the animal appeared to be the opposite to Flyover—mulish, lazy, and reluctant to grab hold of his bridle. I preferred he stayed this way, thinking to myself, I'll give you a couple of right good cracks once we're safely over the first—if we're safely over the first.

The cunning swine must have sensed my intentions for when we approached the fence he jammed his brakes on with no warning and crashed through the wing turning a complete somersault. The last I saw of Jumping Jack was his rear end disappearing over the plough, with my second beloved saddle, stirrup leathers trailing along the ground under his belly.

As I hobbled back towards the changing tent, bruised and sore around the private parts, the Huntsman came cantering along leading Jumping Jack and cradling my totally ruined buckskin over his arm, I shouted, "Don't bring that horse near me, I hate the sight of him." He grinned knowingly and replied, "Pity I bothered to drag him out from the bottom of the open ditch at the South Berks last Saturday."

Hobbling on I spotted Mr and Mrs Percy Pratt running breathlessly towards me. About to give them proper earful, the stupid bitch beat me to the punch and whined, "Thank goodness our Jack is all right, Percy." Completely taken aback all I could muster was, "Eff you and your Jack. I only hope I never clap eyes on you again," before limping away feeling rather sick.

That evening after a good soak in the tub I called Ramsay to tell him the sad story. To make amends he asked me down for a day's hunting with the Puckeridge hounds, my favourite pack, and if I was still suffering from testicular troubles he would provide a side-saddle for me. Before we rang off I told him he was a lousy vet—the chestnut horse, Flyover, made a noise like a grampus, while the bay, Jumping Jack, gurgled like a drowning man.

Not long after this double catastrophe Dick Hern called to suggest we had a day with the Mendip Fox Hounds. He would pick up a couple of hirelings from a local dealer in Exford. I thanked him and said I would have to let him know. Shades of Flyover and Jumping Jack came rushing back!

Should anyone read this story and happen to know the whereabouts of ALD 795 I would be grateful if they would give me a bell.

The completed yard at Wood Farm

Aftermath of War

Twelve months on, when I had gathered together a string of racehorses to train, there was a call from the local stationmaster one dark winter evening. A horse had been consigned to me, he said, and was awaiting collection having been shunted into the sidings. I was expecting no such delivery and therefore hastened to sort out the error.

To my utter amazement, when I shone my torch into the freight wagon I saw none other than Farina, unmistakable because of the corona reale brand on her jowl and her distinctive half tail. Scrawled in chalk on a bit of cardboard attached to her halter were the words: POPE — GORING STATION, ENGLAND.

I was, of course, overjoyed to welcome the old grey mare who was looking tired and weary after her journey from Italy. Her haynet empty and with no water or bedding, she was certainly ready for luxury treatment. The stable yard was full to capacity and therefore my cob had to be relegated to the paddock in order to allow Farina a well-deserved night's rest.

Since she was the wrong sex for a trainer's hack, I decided to breed from her the following spring. Meanwhile Tom Farmiloe, a very good friend, offered to ride her to hounds with the South Berks. Hunting proved an ideal retirement occupation for her and she enjoyed it very much. Alas, one morning she was found asleep in her box: a very peaceful but permanent sleep. Resta in Pace.

FACSIMILE OF MICHAEL POPE'S MC CITATION

25. ARMY TANK BRIGADE... Brigade ...... 7d. DIVISION... Division ......

Schedule No. ......
(to be left blank)

Unit ...... NORTH IRISH HORSE (R.A.C.). ......

Army Number and Rank ...... 217584...... W/LIEUTENANT ......

Name ...... POPE, Michael Bromfield.......
(Christian Names must be stated).

	Brigade Division Corps Army	Honour or Reward	(to be left bl

Action for which commended. (Date and place of action must be stated)	Recommended by.		
On 26 Apr Lieut. M.B. Pope commanded the fwd right tp of 'B' Sqn in the final assault on the DJEBEL RHAR. During the course of this successful action which finally placed LONG STOP in our hands, Lieut Pope's troop silenced seven L.Gs and captured an 88 m.m. A/Tk gun intact after engaging it from the flank. Over 50 prisoners surrendered to his troop and these he shepherded along for a considerable time before handing them over to the Inf. Throughout this engagement Lieut. Bromfield Pope displayed great initiative and resource. He handled his troop with coolness, daring and judgement and his support of the Inf was magnificent. He also displayed great courage when changing his under L.G. fire and his conduct was an example and inspiration to his troop.	Lieut.-Colonel, D. DAWNAY	M.C.	

Awarded M.C.
L.G. 5.7.43

Recommended
B. Howlett Brig.
3 May 44

FIELD.
27 Apr 43.
CO/TH.

D. Dawnay
Lieut.-Colonel,
Commanding North Irish Horse.

Recommended

Howlett
7 May 43.

Brigadier,
Commander, 25th Army Tank Brigade.

in lieu of

next recommendation
Received.

McApplied
Allen
Lt. GENERAL
G.O.C. in C.
FIRST ARMY

10 MAY 1943

90

GOOD FORTUNE IN TWO WORLD WARS

A lucky mascot of Kaiser Bill was presented to my Father, Alec, by my Mother, Tim when he sailed away to serve in France with the Royal Artillery in the first world war in 1918. Both Alec and Kaiser Bill returned home unscathed having survived many bloody battles under inhuman conditions.

Twenty-one years later in 1939 it was my turn to go to war and Alec loaned me his treasured possession to bring me luck. I mislaid the mascot twice in action but thankfully it cast up again and accompanied me home in one piece, although somewhat more scruffy.

Sadly, but peacefully, Alec died at 82 years of age. He was a lovely man whom I admired and respected so much. When sorting through his belongings in a state of grief, for some inexplicable reason, on impulse I threw the little stuffed mascot out to burned with a pile of personal letters and papers.

With a sudden pang of remorse I rushed to the bonfire in the vegetable garden now billowing with smoke and flames. Thank God, Colin, one of my most respected stable lads, stood by clutching a rather dusty and singed Kaiser Bill. Colin remarked, "Somehow the scruffy little fella looked too special to destroy and so I raked him back from the ashes."

Old Kaiser Bill is still with me. I hope and pray he never has to accompany another member of the Pope family to war and when I finally fall off my perch I am certain one of my family will give him a good home and not allow him to suffer the ungrateful fate I so very nearly bestowed upon him.

RECIPE FOR OMELETTE CONFITURE

...as enjoyed by (left to right) Dick Hern, Mike Pope and John Behr.

3 eggs for 5 people (more if hungry)
15 oz. sugar
0.5 oz. sifted flour
A little grated lemon peel
A pinch of salt
1.5 oz. butter

Separate the egg yolks and whites. Put sugar and yolks in a basin and beat. Sprinkle in the flour and continue beating. Beat the egg whites until stiff and fold into yolk mixture. Heat the butter in an omelette pan and pour in the mixture. Put the omelette pan into an oven and cook the mixture for 12/15 minutes. Slide onto a heated dish, spread with jam (strawberry or raspberry), fold over. Sprinkle the surface with sugar and mark with a red hot skewer in a cross-cross pattern burning the sugar, and serve immediately.

INDEX

Ada (family cook at
Thremhall Priory), 9
ALD 795 (the author's
Austin 7), 83, 85, 88
Alexander, General, 36
Algiers, 24, 26, 48, 49
Armstrong, Sam, 11

Barclay family, 1
Barclay, Major Maurice, 4
Beaufort, The Duke of
(Household Cavalry
troop leader), 22
'Beetle', the (Dick Hern's
home-made racing
saddle), 73
Behr, John, 48, 61, 74, 92
Beja, 26
Beyfus KC, Gilbert
(defends Michael Pope
in Jockey Club libel
action), 19
Birkett KC, Norman
(Defence Counsel for
the Jockey Club), 19
Bishops Stortford College,
16
Bowring, Dick, 32
Brown, Graham, 53
'Bullsprick', the (a pliant
cosh as wielded by Dick
Hern), 73

Canadian Infantry
Brigade, 2nd, 49
Canadian Seaforth
Highlanders, 49
Carter, Fanny, 3

Cesena, 60, 76
Churchill Tanks, 24, 34, 40,
44
Churchill, Randolph
(inspects the wounded
author), 30-32
Churchill, Winston, 30, 61
Colin (the stable lad who
thoughtfully rescued
Kaiser Bill, q.v.), 91
Cooper, Basil, 73, 77
Cundell, Frank, 11

Dawnay, Colonel David,
Officer Commanding
the North Irish
Horse, 24, 25, 35, 42,
44, 46, 47, 51
Dick McCreery Cup, The,
79
Dietrich, Marlene, 33
Digby, George, 15
Djebel Ahmera, 36, 38
Djebel Rhar, 34, 36, 38, 42,
44, 46
Dolphin Square
Swimming Baths, 18

Finch-Noyes, Tony, 63, 71,
75
Franklin, Geoff, 51
Harry Hall
(sporting outfitters), 3
Hern, Major Richard
'Dick', i, 29, 35, 48, 60-
61, 63, 67, 72-74, 76-77,
79, 81, 88, 92

Herrin, Flight Lieutenant
'Red', 58
Hewart, Lord Chief Justice
(presided at Jockey
Club libel case), 19
Hitchcock, The Duchess of
('Nicotine Nellie'), 5
Hitler Line, Battle of the,
49, 57

Horses:
'B 37', 22
Birdbrook, 11-12
Birdcatcher, 77
Dormitory, 3, 15, 18
Farina, 60-61, 71-72, 75, 89
Flyover, 87
Ginger, 2, 4, 5, 8
Lot 140, Gallant, 12
Lot 141, Rompsworthy, 12
Mollie, 2, 8
Nera, 60, 61
Pelham Queen, 14
Pitter-Pat, 71, 73, 79, 81
Red Sails, 62, 71, 79, 80, 82
Rhami, 60, 61
Stubbles, 71
Tedeschi, 60, 61
The Bastard, 2
The Masher, 2

Horse & Jockey
pub at Chilton, 17
hot jam omelettes, 48,
Household Cavalry, The,
20, 22
Hughes, Padre, 56

Jockey Club, 19 (libel
action), 74, 85

Kaiser Bill (the author's
lucky mascot), 91
Ketchells, Bill, 29
King, Dick (wireless
controller), 55
King's Dragoon Guards,
16/5th, 60
Knightsbridge Barracks, 20
Kurasov, General (his faux
pas at the Schonbrunn
Palace), 81

Le Keffe, 25
Life Guards, The, 20
Lire Valley, 58
Little Hallingbury Hall, 2
Llewellyn-Palmer, Tony,
58, 60, 70, 73, 77
Longstop Hill, 34, 36, 43,
44, 48, 49
Loot (Barry Pope's
Alsatian dog), 66
Lynn, Vera, 33

Marshall, Mr (the Pope
family's groom), 1-3, 8
McCreery, General
Richard, 77, 79-81
Mendip Fox Hounds, 88
Military Cross (the
author's award and
citation), 46, 90
Miller, Ramsay, 85
Monastery Hill (Monte
Cairo), 58
Mussolini, Benito, 61
NAAFI, 25, 45
Nicholson, Frenchie, 85

North Irish Horse, 24, 27, 29, 36, 46, 47, 58, 64, 65, 73, 74, 77, 81

O'Hare, Sergeant Ted, 39
O'Leary, Paddy, 16
O'Neil, Colonel Lord Shayne, 47

Payne-Galway, Brigadier Peter, 80
Philippeville, 24, 25, 26
'Pizzle' see also 'Bullsprick', 74
Pope, Alec (the author's father), 1, 10, 12-13, 15, 91
Pope, Barry, 60, 62-67, 68-71, 73, 74, 76-77, 79, 81
Pope, Kay (née Long, Mrs Michael Pope), 18, 37, 46-47, 85
Pope, Patrick (the author's twin brother), 1
Pope, Peter (the author's elder brother), 18
Pope, 'Tim' (the author's mother), 2, 5, 9, 10, 12, 13, 91
Poupart, Regimental Corporal Major, Royal Horse Guards, 26, 27, 33
Puckeridge Hunt, The, 1, 6, 13, 88

Ravenna racecourse, 71
Red Cross, The, 56
Reed, Robin, 15
Rew, Major John, 26, 28-29

Rimell, Fred, 11
Rimini, 60, 63, 65, 68, 71, 76, 77
Roscoe Harvey, Brigadier, 80
Rose, Marigold, 6, 7, 8, 13, 14, 15
Rose, Monty, 6, 7, 13, 14
Royal Horse Guards, 20, 26
Russell, Major Gordon, 36, 50, 54, 56

S.S. Duchess of York, 24
Seaforth Highlanders, 49, 52, 55
Simmonds, Reggie (Master of the Berks and Bucks Stag Hounds), 13
Sporting Life, The, 19

Tattersalls (sale at Knightsbridge Green), 10, 11
Teboura, 34
Thremhall Priory (the author's childhood home), 2, 3, 14
Tunis, 34, 38, 44

Victor Emmanuel III, King of Italy, 61, 62
Vienna Racecourse 79
Windsor Park guard duty, 22, 84

Winter, Fred, 11
Wood Farm, 88